ARRIVAL PRESS

POETRY WORKS

I

First published in Great Britain in 1992 by
ARRIVAL PRESS
3 Wulfrick Square, Bretton,
Peterborough, PE3 8RF

All the poems in this book are
printed on 100% recycled paper.

III

Contents

V

VIII

It Looked Like Rain

It looked like rain that
summer's day as she tripped
along the street, and her tiny
shoes beat a sharp tattoo on
the pavement 'neath her feet,
when around the bend came the
man, her friend, in his sleek
and shiny car, and as he caught
her eye he stopped right by and
whispered 'There you are'.

She clambered in and shyly
turned and smiled as off they
sped, as a lilting tune
encompassed them sung by
'Simply Red'. The trees
flashed by and road and sky
merged as if as one, and her
small hand was lost in his as
they journeyed on and on.

They travelled far in the
silver car, and stopped only to
dine, on succulent prawns from
the deep blue sea and sweet
white German wine, and just as
in a fairy tale the scene began
to blur, but envious eyes
around them were aware of him
and her. But both were quite
oblivious of the people sitting
there, for they were in a time
warp that only two can share.

At length he rose to pay the
bill, and she prepared to
leave, and as he strode towards
the door, she clung on to his

sleeve. Outside the light was
diamond bright, as sparkling as
the wine, and they laughed and
cuddled closer as they walked
with arms entwined, to the
waiting motor car into which
they climbed.

Guided by some hand unseen
they chanced upon a pastoral
scene, known perhaps to
Lancelot, a replica of Camelot.
To intensify the strange
illusion a castle lay in deep
seclusion, abandoned by it's
Knights of old, it slumbered
wrapped in mist and cold, as if
under a Merlin spell, a place
where no one cared to dwell.

And here it was, amongst such
splendour, his kiss was gentle,
warm and tender, as she had
know that it would be from
such a caring man as he.
    Barbara Wiltshire

He Spent Ten Pounds

He spent ten pounds on tablets
In several scattered Chemist shops
Not knowing what he'd need
To make his stomach bleed;
Bought water from a supermarket
Chose a secluded, sheltered spot
Determined he would take the lot;
Attempted to - but fell asleep
Awoke, to take some more (and weep).

The chill would bite, he'd turn to stone
He never felt so much alone:
Picked himself up from the floor
And struggled back to his front door.
   M. R. Bell

Michael Bell is a Bradfordian who began writing ten years
ago after coming across the poems of Edward Thomas. His
first collection of poems entitled 'Across the Broad Ford'
was published in 1991.

Reflection

The silence of the poet,
Dancing with words,
Gently waltzing through a maze,
Of colour, light and sound,
Caressing the lines,
With a lover's tenderness,
A thief of hearts with a silver quill,
A judge of contradiction,
Finely threading words,
Into a tapestry of passion,
A stealer of image,
Stabbing at the lines,
A solid, true conviction,
An assassin of art.
Tears fall on the paper,
Washing the page with fear,
Anger sweeps across the canvas,
With colours of hate,
Passion bleeds with every stroke,
Cutting the world into unfamiliar forms,
A jester playing to an open court,
With a demon dance and weary song.
   A. E. Collins

A. E. Collins was born in 1967 and has travelled extensively throughout Europe, Africa and the Middle East. He currently lives in Scotland and hopes to publish a collection of short stories and poetry shortly.

Aftermath

I lie on the cold grey earth
I cannot stand
I have no legs
I gaze up at a black sky
I turn onto my belly
I crawl slowly over the ground
I suck up the mud for sustenance
I have no teeth left
I cannot chew, there is nothing to chew
I have hands but no fingers
I was beautiful a long time ago
I was tall, slim and blonde
I have no hair now
I'm glad we won the war.
   O. J. Palmer

O. J. Palmer was born in London in 1919. She has scribbled poems for fun but this is her first time published. The mother of six children, her hobbies include knitting and gardening.

Jack

My eyes close to the sound of misery,
a closed world
phantom shrieks
pain of undescribable imagination,
an ignorant society
based on T.V. programmes,
Fashion and image conscious people
let's turn the needy onto the streets,

out of sight, out of mind,
no time to stop,
the clock's still ticking
my heart's still beating,
I am all right Jack.
   Richard Thomas

Richard Thomas was born in Whaplode, Lincolnshire in 1966,
and moved to Shirebrook in 1968 where he spent his
childhood until the age of 13, when he moved to Anglesey
where he still lives today.

The Chosen Few

What is it that makes a Manx woman or man
It's hard to define I'll explain it if I can
You must have that seed buried deep within your heart
It's a desperate longing when you are apart
From the place that you love, a sixth sense that you feel
Nostalgia when looking from headlands at Peel.

The beach at Port Greenaugh, Port Soderick and such
The coast down to Langness that means so much
It's a walk through the Baldwins on a warm summers day
The attraction of rabbits espied on the way
Lush green of the valley that falls down below
The grandeur of 'Tholty' when covered in snow

Ayres that give pleasure with sugar fine sand
The knowing that here is the touch of God's hand
A coastline oft rugged, a sea oh so blue
Conviction that it was put there just for you
The splendour of Snaefell as you stand up there
As if you're alone in a world without care.

Is the sound that you hear carried up from the sea?
Or your soul crying out nearer my God to thee
The hills and the slopes, plantations of trees
The urge to give thanks to Him down on your knees
For allowing you the privilege he can
Of being a chosen Manx woman or man.
　Frank Daugherty

Frank Daugherty is Manx born and still lives on the island.
An ex-Merchant seaman, he is now semi retired. He has
written numerous poems and some short mystery stories
due for publication.

An Ode to Susan (and an apology)

The sun shone whilst we were together,
although there were patches of inclement weather.
Sadly, unforeseen threats of a heavy monsoon
drenched me with bitterness and gave rise to the moon.

You shroud me with darkness with your cold resolved mind,
dampening my hopes, making the sun harder to find.
Plagued with suffering through your brave revolt
you've slowly closed the door and secured the bolt.

It's really cold and lonely out in the rain,
and it's freezing knowing the door is never to open again.
A long romance is being washed away with unbearable pain,
like rain water gushing down a roadside drain.

Do you feel the passion in the torture of this ode,
as I sit here abandoned in our abode.
You reside now unperturbed in a place of borrowed exile
with me in my emotional prison with an unobliging file.

The harsh reality has hit me once more,
repression has given me the manners of a boar.
A thirst for revenge blights my aching mind,
but despite what you have done I can't be unkind.

I have pleaded and begged you to have me back
but I know it's hopeless as there is something I did lack,
the love for you was the feeling seldom expressed,
and as a result I am now lonely and depressed.

I wish you fulfilment despite my mocks
and hope you sail away with a better ship from the docks.
Leave me waving good wishes to you,
for that new found lover should bear something new.
   Dennis John Kirk

Dennis Kirk was born in North Battersea in 1954. He comes
from a working class background and is currently employed
in the engineering trade. In his spare time he writes poetry
and hopes one day to have them published.

The World

When I woke up the world seemed so clean
The grass was green
The sky so blue
Just waiting there for me and you
But to think I could end with
A flick of a switch
One government disagreeing
With another
It makes me feel sick.
   Darren Graham Rigden

Darren Rigden lives in Eastleigh, he is 26 years old and
this is his first poem to be published.

Sir Winston Churchill's Statue

An effigy so powerful
Of a man does tell
Hard he worked and hard he schemed
To serve his country well
Sir Winston Churchill's watchful eye
His statue does portray
Overlooking Parliament
In no uncertain way.
   Melvyn Roiter

Melvyn Roiter was born in Hampton Court, Twickenham,
in 1940. He now lives in Romford and is a freelance writer
and London Cabby. A selection of his London poems have
been featured on television and in the press.

Oblivion Bound

Oblivion calls as we steer the course;
Through the wet windy channels of a coast which we force,
To hate us as much as Hades, so much that our bodies
Are hardened and our voices are hoarse - as we work
To the time that we'll feel the remorse
For wiping down engines is the job that I do
My life is so small profiteering for who?
Have you been watching the world cup and the motif they
                                                    show
National Power the anthem, your friend but our foe.
For this is the firm that sends us to sea
And away from our homes where'er they may be.
And at the end of our time when we're good for no more
They throw us ashore to drink and to whore
And at the end of our wedge of money we go,
Back to the life breeding bitterness so;
The next time you come across a seaman so tight
That you never did think that you'd see such a sight.

Think of the world cup and wimbledon and strawberries and
                                                  cream
And then think of the men to whom these things are a
                                                  dream
So don't think him a drunk who wets his own bed
But think of the life in the past he has led
And then think of his future and the things it will hold
And know that tho' drunk, will dry up and face bold
Whether it be keeping the National Grid running for you
Or change his firm and location, doing whatever for who.
    Raymond Thorne

Ray Thorne lives in London and this is his first published
work.

Waking

Waking in the night,
I see you standing there.
A black silhouette.
Standing there, waiting for me.
Stretching out my hand,
I reach for you,
With longing and with love.
Reaching for the impossible
The unattainable.
Reaching for the dream.
But you're not there.
Only empty blackness.
You're not there,
And knowing that,
Again I die, a little.
Again I die.
    Shirley Lloyd

Shirley Lloyd was born in Birmingham but now lives in
Scotland. She has only just begun to write poetry.

Homosapiens

Sometimes I sit and wonder,
My mind in full flight, in a canter
Starting from a standing start
Searching for answers which we cannot seem to find.
Beyond limits of our comprehension,
Beyond the boundaries of our understanding.
The expanding vastness of the universe
Cannot match the corners I stretched my mind.
To find answers which eluded me,
Theories that constantly confused me.
Man, power of articulate speech,
Abstract reasoning, imagination and greed.
Help me if you can,
Explain the paradox
Unpredictabliity of man.
   Michael Stephenson

Michael Stephenson was born in London of Jamaican
parentage. He attended Russell High School in Jamaica and
Harrow College of Higher Education. He writes short stories
and poetry which he hopes to publish.

The Common Market

Now what is wrong with fish and chips
wrapped in a newsy scene
Why should we use the camouflage
that other countries seem
to thrive on; I don't care if I should
lose the 'Frenchies' handshake
For I likes me drink in glasses,
not soaking in me pancake.
So you can keep your crepe suzette
and hope your soufflé rises
If I wants a steak, I cooks a steak,
not warm meat in disguises.

I'll have cods roe not caviar
and greens instead of saukraut
And me rice I'll have as pudding
washed down by ale or stout.
At least I know it's not been made
by help of people's feet
In shoes and socks they pick the hops
Me grapes I likes to eat.
So I'll have boiled beef and carrots
and I'll thrive on mutton stew
No bolognaise nor pasta will I gorge
And I'll leave it to Antonio
to toast with macaronio
I toast with roast beef -
England and St. George.
    Pam Owers

Pam Owers lives in Cranham, writing poetry is just a hobby
to her.

Dedication to the Miners

The miners lamp is gleaming bright
To guide them night and day
And the son of God, Jesus Christ
Will lead them all the way

There are many miners who toil beneath the earth
If you know a miner you know what he's worth
Some miners dig for diamonds, silver, tin or gold
But many of the miners they bring out the coal.

They toil and work very hard
To give energy to our land
For the comfort of a cosy fire
There is no magic wand.

No miner wants to be on strike or misunderstood.
All he wants to do is work to earn his livelihood
And in the bleak midwinter when the earth is hard as ice
Look at your cosy fire burning warm and bright

For this I thank a miner and I say well done
You have earned your reward, you've earned it by the ton.
    B. Cooley

Untitled

When darkness surrounds,
Open your eyes and you will
See me. And if your loneliness
Prevails, reach out your arms,
and you will find me.

For through the storms and turmoil,
A calm shall be paramount within
Fragile walls of comfort.

And when all else fails,
I will still be there;

For I have journeyed.
And I know suffering too.
    C. L. McRitchie

Claire McRitchie is 21 years old and lives in Birmingham.
She hopes to have a collection of poems published shortly.

Why?

Why do I still love you
When you treat me so bad,
Why did you break my heart
And leave me feeling so sad?

Why did you pick me
From all the others you could get
Why did you leave
And of my love forget?

Why don't you come back
And let us try again
Why can't you see
Your love will ease my pain?

Why do you smile
Across the room to me
Why are you dancing
Here, now, for everyone to see?

Why do you hold me
So very close to you
Why do you care of
My feelings are true?
    Elaine Timney

Elaine Timney lives in Glasgow and is a full time
telephonist. She has enjoyed writing poetry for a number
of years.

Dear Grandma

So you've retired, so what!
All the time in the world you've got
Grandma can you have the kids?
While we go and visit Sid's
Will you have the cats next week?
Let the plumber in to mend a leak.
The ironing's right up to the sky
Can you do it when you come by,
Dear Grandma you are so good
Call at the market for some food,
Would you like to come and stay
And mind the house while we're away

Keep grandma going, she will keep fit
She doesn't mind, no not a bit
It's nice to be wanted and loved by all
And to be at everyone's beck and call
    T. Hynes

The Old Man

The lonely figure sits on the bench
The rain falls hard and he gets drenched
He has not eaten for many a day
And the passers by just go their own way
None of them know of the hurt and the pain
This old man has suffered again and again
How he lost his wife
The person he loved
How on that fatal day last week
God took her above
No one can hear the cry in his heart
Now that his life has crumpled apart
Because of the rain there is not a trace
Of the tears that roll
Down the old man's face
That lonely figure just sits on the bench
The rain falls hard, and he gets drenched.
    Colleen Knight

Colleen Knight was born in Folkestone in 1958. Life itself
plays a great part in her writing and she has a good many
poems which she hopes to get published soon.

Autumn

When the leaves begin to fall,
All over the floor
If I could pick them up,
And stick them back
To where they were before.
Well there would be nothing to explore
Nature is a gift of God
To live for evermore.
    Florence Clara Garner

Florence Garner was born in 1915. One of ten children, she married and had five children of her own, with no time to study or relax. Now, at 76 years of age she has taken up poetry.

Thoughts in the Sistine Chapel

Beauty is here that never palls,
And one in wonder can but stare
Upon the decorated walls
And marvel at the glory there;
Then to the ceiling turn the gaze
Where art and brilliant colour blend,
And ponder on those bygone days
When Michaelangelo did wend
His way to where we now do stand
To weave his magic in the place,
And raise this monument so grand
To Church and to the Holy Grace.
    George L. Naylor

George Naylor is a retired government officer born in Yorkshire. He now resides in London and writes as a hobby.

The Bomb

The moon may rise, the sun may set,
But man the bomb will soon regret,
It's small in size but large in power
Destroying towns within an hour.

The death is quick for soon you feel
The pain of skin that starts to peel,
Too late to pray too late to cry
For now you know you're bound to die.

Now powers of the world take heed
Of nuclear war the demon's seed,
Father, mother, sister, brother,
Soon your lands, your lives they'll smother.
   Colin Mackie

Colin Mackie is an amateur artist and animator. He has
written various articles in his previous work in researching.
He hopes to write many more poems possibly on his native
city of Glasgow.

The Butterfly

I've started as a caterpillar
Long and fat, with hair
I turn into a crysalis
On a branch, I'm hanging there.

Inside my cocoon, I'm a grub,
Waiting for my season
It's nature so I'm being told,
There is no other reason.

The time has come, I've got to stretch,
And break out of my shell
Am I a moth or a butterfly,
Only time will tell.

Well, I am out, so pretty and so slender,
A lovely pattern on my back
At least I know I'm not a moth
And I'm pretty glad of that!
  S. M. Welsh

Mandy Welsh is an insurance administrator who resides in
Brighton, Sussex but is originally from Ashford in Kent. This
is her first attempt at writing poetry.

The Spinney

The sun glares down on beaten stones,
As on old and wizened bones.
Weeds cover every crack
Everywhere under attack.

Timbers hang loose and ill
Sigh and fall at will
Testament of decay
From a forgotten day.

Through the broken panes
Bespattered by repeating rains
We see the bleakness unfold
Kin to damp and mould.

Broken hinges moan
That they cannot condone
Neglect and disarray
That somebody should pay.

A beauty that has run to waste,
Bad fruit to leave a bitter taste.
But hope does survive
That someone will revive

This dank and dusty pile
To it's former style
That now only spiders know
As they watch their cobwebs grow.
   Mandy Mayes

Mandy Mayes is a secretary born in Chelmsford, now living
in Holland-on-Sea where she writes for her own pleasure.
She is a cat and history lover and enjoys reading as well
as writing.

You

You, wherever you are,
In need I call your name
In doubt I hide with fear,
Was it all a game, I ask
Were we just a little insincere
Why did you say goodbye?
I question, within my mind,
With every tear I long for you
But want cannot provide alone.

Please somebody, take this pain away
It's getting deeper and deeper
I'm wading through a sea of sorrow
Desperately seeking peace of mind.
I'll always remember you my friend
One day without the pain
But I'll always miss your company
Again and again and again...
   Yvonne Rayner

My Love Lost

Without you my world is non-existent
A naked and forlorn wasteland
Deserted because of wounds self-inflicted
An open hole that no one could fill.

I am void of warmth and understanding
Which, dear one, you so freely gave to me
Now sad and lorn while in this prison
Because of an error, a fool perpetrated

I am now a picture of decrepit being
When you were always there beside me
I felt alive, like I was happy - volant
But now I live the life of the lifeless

Maybe one day, our paths will cross
You and I, dear one, will walk together
We will accrete, never to be parted
Until we are called to new life beyond.
   Stuart John Wilding

Stuart Wilding was born in Blackpool in 1953, a painter and
decorator by trade he has also written poems and short
stories under the pen name of Stuart Stephenson.

I See a Man

I see a man
His face shrouded in greed
Who likes to think he owns
All that he sees

Close behind him
A dark shadow follows
Urging him to sell
That which is only borrowed

His hands dipped in the blood
Of those who stood in his way
A glint behind his feral eyes
His evil emotions betray

Without a second thought
He takes and rapes the land
The land that God gave
To each and every man.
   Gary Kenyon

Gary Kenyon lives in Hull. Although he has written several poems this is the first time he has submitted anything for publication.

Valentine

You were my Valentine
And then
I lost the love
I was dreaming of

You went your way and forced me to mine
Why do things change
Dear Valentine

From this sweet love came peace within
And then
It is over, separate lives begin

I tried so hard to adjust with time
Lonely without my Valentine

But from this love came something more
I have the best friend, whom I adore

A love that is lost heals with time
No more to be my Valentine

I will love you always with my heart
In the future
Today
Just like from the start.
   Rosemarie Lockyer

Rosemarie Lockyer ws born in Cornwall in 1957. She writes
for a hobby and this is the first of her work to be submitted
to a publisher.

The Tale of the Invisible Knight

The Knight was a beast who knew only hate,
But something occured which had changed him of late.
'What's happening here' the knight did say,
'What causes my form to be seen in the day?'
The answer was easy, as well he knew,
Would never dare even be guessed by so few.
The love for a woman who he never could see,
For much though he loved her it would never be.
The risk of his capture had torn him apart,
For he knew this young lady had taken his heart.

To offer his love or surrender his passion,
To deliver his heart unto her was his mission.
While the darkness of hell was the home of his thoughts,
The light from her heart was the heaven he sought.
His every waking moment both in the dark or light,
To seek her love; a quest for her, through either day or
                                                  night.
But could such a beast ever hope to be tamed,
By the beautiful rose that the dark man had named.
The knight's only flaw was his inhuman side,
Could it ever be buried; as it never would hide.

As her class was so high she felt she was above him,
Could love cross such boundaries; would she ever love him?
Might her love entrap him and bind him in chains,
Thus destroying the beast, leaving human remains.

So this image of her which was stuck in his head,
Of her pale skin so smooth and her full lips so red.
The way she sat still as he pictured her there,
With those deep sea blue eyes and that flowing brown hair.
His undying love like the flames that keep burning,
But afraid she's gone now with no hope of returning.
  R. P. Daley

Raymond Daley was born in Coventry in 1969. He is a keen
runner and is currently working for the government. This
is his first published work.

Gambler's Lament

He walked into the betting shop, a white and tight cheeked
                                                      face,
He is one of life's big losers, in the hard run human race.
He is one of oh so many that find the going hard
And he tries to hide his worries in the daily racing card.

Today's the day! (he thinks) as he surveys the motley crew,
He's forgotten yesterdays losers, as he tries to pick a few,
It's hard to kick the habit, he's tried in many ways
But it's only himself he's fooling if he thinks that gambling
                                                      pays.

Why is it so destroying, why is it such a drug
Why does it make a sensible man act just like a simple
                                                      mug?
It's hard to face the truth, they say, it more than often
                                                      hurts,
But nothing turns your stomach more than losing all these
                                                      'certs'.

To pick a winning Yankee is the punters one big aim
But two will fall, one get pipped and the other one go lame,
'I'll pick the favourite in this race, he'll win it by a mile'
But it's just another loser, he tries to raise a smile.

'My luck's bang out I couldn't win an argument (He whispers
                                         to his mate),
Everything I back - seems to be carrying over weight.
'Where will my next win come from? I haven't got a clue
But if things don't change, I don't know what I'm going to
                                         do.'

I've seen the self destruction that's gone on through the
                                         years,
The heartbreak and the misery, the break-ups and the tears
What is the answer to this craving, what do you have to
                                         do?
There isn't a simple solution, it's really down to you.
    E. Aston

Child of Love

Nine long months were not in vain
you kicked and sometimes gave me pain
but you were worth it child of love
someone to cuddle, someone to hug.
Oh, pretty baby from my womb
Small and soft and tender
your tiny hand I hold today
this first day of December.
You wince and give a little sigh
and hour of your life's gone by,
finding out things strange and new
your future lies ahead of you.
Darling a daddy you will never see
he left me and deserted thee
but do not fret my little son
we'll cross life's hurdles one by one.
    Jean Wilcock

Margaret Jean Wilcock was born in North Shields in 1953.
Now living in Nottingham, she writes poetry as a hobby and
hopes it gives enjoyment to others.

Such is Life

Behind the railroad track on that lonely hill,
Came the Kelly Gang, the police were calm and still
The shots rang out along the valley floor
And the Kelly Gang drew their guns once more.

The boys went down one by one
A heart once beating, extinguished by a gun,
Ned came forth and his armour shone
Soon he would be the only one.

Glenrowan town was that fateful place,
The police met Ned face to face
They always knew he was going to hang
They always wanted that Irish man.

Ned was trapped, nowhere to go,
Face was stern, no emotion to show,
Nothing to say, coy little smile,
Australia's son of the Emerald Isle.

Melbourne gaol last saw Ned alive,
Heart stopped beating at twenty five,
Hung him by the neck until he was dead,
Such is life is all he said.
   Lee James Nelson

Lee Nelson lives in Stockton-on-Tees, Cleveland. Although
his works have still to be published several have been
performed by him as songs on stage abroad.

Freedom Road is Stained with Blood

Freedom road, is this the way it should be,
It's the children who suffer, segregation,
Walls of fear are walls of tears.
A society bred to fear and hate
the first sad step,
Freedom road is stained with blood
The innocent. the dispossesed,
the bombed out houses, silent streets.
Freedom road, is this the way it should be.
    Mark Carroll

Mark Carroll was born in Waterford in 1966. After living
a number of years in England he returned to Ireland where
he now writes full time.

Sympathetic Appetite

Sunday in the countryside
Brought squeals of sheer delight
The interest was a little lamb
With a nose as black as night.

Kiddies tried to stroke his back
Then feed him sugar cane
They said his woolly coat was soft
And hoped it wouldn't rain.

Mothers showed their tender thought
And gave him much affection
When children tried to pinch his nose
They got the right correction.

Now Father with his baccy pouch
When filling up his pipe
Agreed with all the family
The lamb's a pretty sight.

Auntie said that poets
Wrote of him in verse
If anyone should hurt him
Would surely bring a curse.

Cousin Bill had warned them
A dog was near at hand
And to save the pet from danger
They would form a fighting band.

Alas the time for parting
Was a very sorry sight
Pity for the little one
Went on throughout the night.

The following day was gloomy
And worked against the will
They hoped that goodness would prevail
That the pet was happy still.

All the week it went on
Of the creature near the ridge
But mother got the topic
In the inside of her fridge.

And so to Sunday day of rest
By now I'm sure you will have guessed
With table minus cheese and jam
The plates are full of lovely lamb.
    E. Wood

E. Wood is an ex-desert rat, now retired. Lived in Coventry
for over fifty years, a few poems published, now working
on a book.

Why?

Oh why did I agree
To work in trendy infants
Where the chaos
Is not organised
As upstairs?

Don't use the sand as snuff
Don't tip the water trough
Leave the wool and other fluff
And you've had paint enough
Please don't go in a huff!

Oh, why did I leave
My calm and orderly routine
To work in trendy infants
Where chaos reigns
Supreme?

No 'hit the letter' doesn't mean
Wallop the computer screen!
And don't have an accident I know you're keen!
Oh dearie me, he's turning green
It's only plasticene.

Why, I ask myself
It's clear
No one
Else
Would!
  Bindi Routledge

Bindi Routledge has been teaching in Glasgow for sixteen
years. Until now her writing and accompanying illustrations
have appeared in school productions.

My Figure

Oh I wish I'd looked after my figure
It just seems to get bigger and bigger
I've tried all the diets, and weight watchers too
I've even tried starving but it makes me feel blue
(Oh I wish I'd looked after my figure).
I lie in bed at night, like a blown up kite
When I look in the mirror I do look a sight
I run up and downstairs, like a silly clown
Instead of a smile I now wear a frown
(Oh I wish I'd looked after my figure)
When I think of the chocolates and cream buns I ate
I can't run for a bus because of my weight
When I open my wardrobe and see my nice clothes
When will they fit me, God only knows
(Oh I wish I'd looked after my figure)
    C. Balmain

Catherine Balmain is a senior citizen from Glasgow who
writes verses for a hobby.

Power

Mottled colours, green and blue
Sparkling as the morning dew,
The wavelets, stretching from the beach
To distant lands far out of reach,
Beyond horizons faintly showing
In the sunset painted, glowing,
Further round along the bay,
Rocks and cliffs now worn away,
By tireless action of the tide
From which no mortal thing can hide,
A force with mighty awesome power,
Never ceasing every hour,
It's part of the eternal plan
Which regulates the life of man,
The power that hovers all around

To keep our feet upon the ground,
Changes day to darkest night,
With pictures etched by starry light,
Yet in this world where we are thrust
There is a feeling of mistrust,
Nations take revenge on others
Instead of talking peace with brothers,
When will we learn to live in peace,
Until our earthly travels cease.
    L. Kirkland

Leonard Kirkland was born at Ibstock, Leics., in 1923. After
war service with the Royal Signals he married and settled
in Sheffield. Now physically handicapped he is writing his
life story in verse.

October

Shadowed fronds of autumn beckon
From darkening corners of the night.
Chillness drifts in with the sea mists,
Clasping summer's fading light.

All around a passive silence,
As nature carpets up her floor;
Sedated beauty softly drifting
Now autumn opens up her doors.

October - with a web of colour
Spins her autumn tapestry.
Morning skies are flush with treasures;
Sunset roses stain the seas.
    Malcolm Wilson Bucknall

Malcolm Wilson Bucknall was born in Nottingham in 1935.
He is an ex-coal miner, ex-merchant seaman and club
steward. He has had over one hundred and fifty of his poems
published.

Inspirational Ways

A job or two perhaps
Certainly a caution to take
Similarly I could bear not
One individual depending on his
Self inspiration and motivation.
Developing an ability so great
To withdraw such an attention.
A formidable power of such
Consistency witheld in the mind
and total mental ability.
Stability, equilibrium, balance the thought
a just way to your physical attitude as well.
Helping you through a mascara of daily
demands and persistency to develop yourself
properly. No circumstances of any kind
Spoiling your way of working so hard.
Inspiring and amending ways, which, never
dealt with. A built driving force
Consistency gets you the favoured post.
Forever and more. Willingly you develop further,
more. Into a high demanding situation
A step higher or two.
A brilliant episode of unlawly miscarriage or two.
What efforts, so put rightly away
A maximum scoring to a happy and tireless
Work day.

One may say human consumption.
Takes what's there.
Though in one's mind or mine
I think truly and say one person, could improve
putting a mind to work.
And remember, cherish a forthcoming ways of
developing, travelling further to a wisk of
tremendous abilities.
Unknown to you.
  S. Rahman

Syedur Rahman lives in Luton, Bedfordshire. His hobbies are writing poetry and stamp collecting.

The Lost Child

Standing in a corner,
lonesome and forlorn
No one here to love me
No one who can care.
I'm the child with clothes in tatters,
I'm the child with stomach thin.
My heart is empty, cold and weak,
My mind is numb, so very numb.
Day after day my life goes on,
Day after day I wish I could die
I've been battered, beaten blue
I've been abused with hatred strong.
Please dear God don't let this go on,
Please dear God treat me in a special way
You put me on this earth for love
You gave me to people, my own family
Take me back to your gentle world
Take me in your strong warm arms.
Enrich my body with street caress,
Enrich my life with your endless love.
Once I was lost, forever lost,
But now I am found, forever found.
    Sonia Binge

Sonia Binge, now aged 24, has lived in Bracknell since the age of five. She works within Social Services and has a special interest in dramatherapy. Until recently she has only written for pleasure.

The Fly

I watched a fly in crazy flight
Around my room, oh, such a sight;
Climbing, darting, why all this
Has his steering gear gone amiss?

I kept on watching with keener glance
Until my eyes did smart and dance,
A teeny-weeny creature he
But how more active than mighty me.

Forward, round and back he jayed,
He didn't want my place in bed,
For never once did he come down
To rest awhile on my eiderdown.

Up and down again he'd lead
A long range flight this was indeed.
'Why don't you rest a while you hound
Is there no landing place to be found?'

I wondered was he watching me
And if he was, what did he see?
Six feet of laziness still in bed,
I'll swear here's what the creature said.

'It's twelve o'clock, pyjama clothes,
You're still in bed, one thing fly loathes
If I was wasp, or even bee
I'd rise you quick my boy, you'd see.'

I got up then but still I mused,
For out of my window the messenger cruised,
He'd done his job, the message made known,
And before I could thank him the fly had flown.
    Andrew Cardwell

Andrew Cardwell was born and has always lived in County Down. Now retired, he occasionally writes poetry for personal and family pleasure. Has had articles published in rural newspapers.

Have You Ever Been To Bethlehem?

Have you ever been to Bethlehem
To see where Christ was born?
Or stood beside the Galilee
And watched the coming morn?
Have you climbed the Mount of Olives
To watch the sun go down
Upon the Holy City?
The Gem of Israel's crown.

Have you walked there in the garden
Where Jesus knelt to pray
Asking God the Father,
To take this cup away?
Have you ever knelt at Calvary
Where they nailed Him to a tree?
The Son of God, the Holy One,
Who died for you and me.

Have you ever been to see the tomb
Wherein His body lay?
Waiting for the resurrection
Of that first Easter Day.
Where angels rolled the stone away
To show that He had risen
And that God had kept His promise
To the world that He had given.
  Maisie Reid

Maisie Reid is a housewife living in Northern Ireland. This poem was written after a visit to the Holy Land in 1988.

A Day in the Country

How nice to feel a meadow
So soft beneath your feet,
Instead of a hard pavement
In a crowded city street.
See a blue bird,
Hear a lark, or a cuckoo in a tree.
Laughing with the children
As they run towards me,
Carrying arms of flowers
Dancing in the sun
We'll make a daisy chain for everyone
Cool rippling waters
Over stones do flow
Children paddling feet, shout 'It's cold as snow'.
'Let's have our picnic now' I say.
We sat on the ground,
Some of us lay.
Bottles of pop, cakes and sandwiches too
An apple, an orange, for you and for you
It's time to go home now
As in our coach we sped
Back to that dreary city
I began to dread.
Then I looked at the children
Handicapped as they were
With their happy smiling faces
You could take them anywhere.
   Margaret Rose Warman

Margaret Warman was born in Birmingham and now lives in Droitwich, Worcs. She works as a nurse and enjoys painting, cake decorating and writing poetry and articles for local newspapers.

The Dead and the Living

I first saw a deceased when I was nine years old, my father said not to worry as the dead are the same as the living, only the laughter has left them, the sparkle has gone from their eyes, the worry has been lifted from their shoulders, and their voice has vanished to eternity.

In paradise the sparkle will return for it is the twinkle of the stars, the laughter will return too for it is the morning breeze and the turning tides are their sides shaking with laughter.

I treat the deceased with the same courtesy as I give to the living, though I find the deceased are always more polite. My father also had a few words to say about the living.

He said that the living are only the caretakers of the soul, yet they think their existence is everything, that they know everything because they experience many things with their senses.

What the living don't acknowledge is that their time is short and when I lay their bodies to rest then their souls continue without them, without their strong, without their weak, without their beautiful or even ugly temporary form, to where I cannot say, only that it is a better place.

Percy, the undertaker placed the lid on the coffin, the soul was free.
    Michael Gerard Casey

Pass On

Dull flesh surrounding tired bone,
earthly life is fleeing fast
Brainpower slowing, thinking, cloudy,
on a track of nothingness.

This state of presence, frame of mind,
from a lengthened life, gets thro' to every kind.
Of people's living, rich or poor,
some have less, others more.

No choice a-given, nor sign revealed
settles at will as twilight seals.
Ere' the after-life doth touch us,
with the promise of eternity.

The world of souls beckoning dreamy,
light pure a fresher air.
No more needing material rendering,
in a newer world a-waiting there.
   N. Rawlinson

Nora Rawlinson is a mature student attending college for
'A' level in art and design. She writes short stories and
poetry in her spare time.

Moment

We sat alone across the unpolished table.
The smoke from our cigarettes curled
playfully as it drifted towards the ceiling.

We were talking quietly of the recent past,
several days had elapsed since we met last.
For the thousandth time we were playing that scene.
Dull grey sound filled the spaces between.
My mind's fist then began to pound
as mediocrity set about dragging us down.

But suddenly, with a mere word or gesture,
your face seemed to peel, layer by stale layer.
Years of familiarity faded away,
as if we'd met for the first time that day.

Life flickered wildly in your cool green eyes.
Your gaze burned through me like a star.
Then, in that frozen moment, I realised
I was seeing you as you always are:
Simply beautiful.
   A. S. Onions

Alan Onions was born in London in 1959. He works as a
computer operator for a large food distribution company and
is currently writing a short story and a novel.

Wayside Pearl

On a sombre, bleak and wintry day,
When the world is seemingly coloured grey,
Stands a tiny flower, so brave and bold
Determined to conquer the interminable cold,

Through snow and ice and frost and mist
These miniscule drops of delight persist
Glistening with the early dew
Forcing us to look at the world anew

What joy to see the wayside pearl,
It's small translucent leaves unfurl,
Coy and discreet in many a hedgerow,
Still dancing as the winter winds blow,

This gentle hint of the season to be
Makes it's presence felt so powerfully
That even the birds appear to sing
The snowdrop, a first brief glimpse of spring.
   Lorraine Saville

Lorraine Saville lives in Newbury and is a product manager for a computer software company. She has been writing poetry as a hobby since childhood, but until now has never considered publication.

Nightmare

Unbidden,
it squirmed thro' the dream in my brain
courage castrated - insane and inane,
infesting, ingesting my very marrow
with it's hypnotic haunting and harrowing barrow
of ice-cold chills
infusing a draught of mind-blowing ills
Consciousness clamped in cryptic strands
creating impotent cataleptic bands with
sepulchral shiver
I sweated a stone
as it slithered and sickened me
down to the bone
It flickered a finger
to the beckoning flames
fascinated feet tottered
in fast forward reply
a frightening role
as a fearsome foreboding
took control of my soul
I was one of the doomed
desperate damned
futilely I fought fate
from Fate's own fangs
the fire licked it's lips
it's breath scorched my throat
all Hell in that smell
I yelled at the smoke
then
I awoke.
   Desmond O'Donnell

Desmond O'Donnell was born in Newark in 1941, now lives in Scotland. Married with two daughters and two dogs, ex-Royal Navy currently working in avionics.

Apartheids Savannah Sun

Black is the heart of the dictators regime
That keeps the pure heart of the black man down,
Under the Savannah plains of the African sun,
Apartheid is their ugly word for segregation of the soul,
Dividing all the fertile lands,
From barren earth the blacks control,
Deep is the vein of bloody hate,
That tributary to river flows,
Long is the stain of carnage red.
That under the African sun onward grows,
Time is the message loud and long,
That beats it's rhythm like tom tom drum,
Fate is the answer all await,
Under the African Savannah sun.
   Ian Towers

Ian Towers was born in Manchester in 1946, he has written an edition of poems entitled 'A Candle Burning Soon', in 1976. He is a member of the Shettlestown Writers Workshop in Glasgow.

Time to See

Ever seen a baby born
Or watched a child die
Ever heard two lovers quarrel
Or heard a mothers sigh

Ever watched a baby grow
Or precious moments floating by
Start to caress a blood red rose
Only to watch it fade and die

Gods green leaves on countless trees
You watch them turn to gold
Winters wand bids them fall
No longer green, now wet and cold.

Can you stop a bloody war
With battles fought in vain
Promises of a better world
Yet things remain the same

What is to be I know will be
Man's efforts oh so frail
We walk this way but only once
Yet leave a bloody trail

Nature knows the only way
Of sunny rays and gentle rain
Someday somehow we will notice
And find our sanity again
    C. Leathem

Cain Leathem is a 22 year old Glasgow born Brummie. He
writes for pleasure and hopes to see more of his work in
print.

Lost in Antrim

A friend moved house to Antrim town
And sent me an invitation
I went along to visit her, but
forget to bring information.
At a gate of an estate - I stood
to wait
In hope that her small son
would find me
Time passed away, and no-one
came,
So I thought I would venture
alone

Over hills and down lanes
To search for her new home
At last to my shock, I suddenly
stopped
To realize that I was lost!
I tried to turn back, but could
not find my track
Over a bank I scrambled,
Suddenly I stumbled, and fell
down a hill
My stocking was torn,
My arm nearly broken
More and more frustrated I came
I asked someone the way, but
he didn't know what to say
So I felt quite alone and forsaken!
I knocked on the door where a taxi
was parked
Back to Belfast he drove
A ten pound fare was what I had to pay
For my venture of the morning
Never again will I go out alone
Without some kind of information.
    Mary McVeigh

Mary McVeigh now lives in Belfast although she originates
from Co. Down. Several of her poems have been published
and she would like to see her own book in print in the
future.

The Humber Bridge

The Humber Bridge is a beautiful construction;
With it's towers stood so bold;
I watched it progress throughout the span
I treasure it like gold.

The building was a family affair
Everyone joined in;

Father, brothers, husband, in-laws,
Working for a sin;
My father lost his life on there:
Had heart attack and died
My god it really broke my heart
The family we all cried;
But then finally on completion day
What a sight to see
The wonderful single span bridge
That means so much to me;

When I sit and view there,
With blue skies on a day
Watch the traffic flowing across
Coming from each way
People, they're just strolling along
Watching the yachtsmen play
Children playing along the shores
Having a lovely day.
   Jean McTaggart

Jean McTaggart was born in Hull in 1954. A voluntary
worker and fundraiser for the disabled, she has been writing
poetry since childhood, recently seeing it appear in local
papers.

Strychnine Youth Riot

bodybag manifesto fires poison dart of party politics
while teenage hallucinations spew rotten debris
judges, teachers, parents, politicians condemn, laugh, mock
while angry youths riot through the cities
burn down the courts and police stations, firebomb the
Houses of Parliament

ultra-violence prevails and war-heroes are trampled
underfoot
Discredited spraypaint slogans ring true
while fat middle-aged music journalists scream
bodies melting in a boiling acid vat of George Michael CDs

Desolation equals broken class rules
and knee-capped junk dealers beg mercy
as their pyramid collapses on them
Burnt out Molotov cocktail generation of emptiness

Culture of nothing
Nothing but hate
   Anthony Melder

Anthony Melder lives in Brentwood, Essex and works for a
design agency near his home. He is currently working on
several short stories and a collection of poems which he
hopes to have published.

The Rising City

The bark echoed a plea
The limbs torn disjointedly entwined the morning sunlight
As the wind resounded it's fear of the concrete army.

Thousands like Kitchener's army rise to meet the battle of
                             day
Artillery-fire traffic rips gaping wounds
Through sombre streets the sound of man at play while the
                             wind
Resounds its fear of the concrete army.

A sparrow's tear is nought to man at play as it writhes
Across a smoke-filled sky.
And as it falls to tree to die
The wind resounds its fear of the concrete army.
   Richard Woollven

Richard Woollven was born in 1951 in London. He has travelled quite widely across the country, mainly living the city life. He hopes to publish his own work soon.

Fireworks

Rockets go bang
Bangers go bump
Things like that
Make you jump.
They fly through the air
It gives you a scare
Mummy mummy
Look up there

Catherine wheels spinning in the night air
Everybody's laughing
But children take care
Sparkling sparklers in your hands
Dancing snowdrops on the sands
Everybody's going
So do take care
See you next year
If you dare.
  Paul Ratcliffe

Paul Ratcliffe is ten years old and was born in Stoke-on-Trent in 1981. He attends St. Paul's School and would like to have more of his work published.

A Highland Journey

Cloudy skies and waters calm bathe the sleepy dawn,
As busy wheels and changing reels excite the early morn,
A morn without concrete mold to obscure the well set scene,
Where mountain air and natures sound does kiss the lazy
stream.

Faster, faster the new age speeds on the country's more
                                          gentle breast
Where babes and kids and adults too witness the old and
                                          news' unrest,
The old with firm identities, the new with brash ideas,
The old steeped in centuries, the new engulfed in fears.
'Animals in a field' cried a wayward well fed child
As if eternities triumphs past were discovered as a new.
Briefly, slowly, rendezvous are made at stages on the way,
And maybe by chance, there is, to glimpse yesterday mourn
                                          today,
New scenes unfold as natures slight of hand does play
Some kind of mystical magical move to give four seasons
                                          in a day.
Suddenly the nest, a whisper travels and welcomes do
                                          abound,
And as they subside, images reside without a trace or sound.
   D. J. Will

David Will was educated in the Orkney Isles and now lives
in East Kilbride due to his work in the civil service. He is
an enthusiastic amateur songwriter.

Mother

Mother had become a burden.
She wet her bed at night.
Went for walks in her night clothes
So they put her in a home.
She was senile or so they said.

Mother didn't understand....
She was frightened.
Mother wept...
Where was she
Who were all these people who slept
Where was her daughter?
The daughter she had carried in her now constipated belly.
Loved dancing feet, pony tails and all
Frank, Frank, but Frank was dead.
Nobody talked, just slept.
So she slept too, it was easier that way.
    K. O. Howard

Karen Howard hopes one day to publish a poetry book
entitled 'Everyday Poems for Everyday People'. She is a
nurse at London's Charing Cross Hospital.

The Little House Where I Was Born

That little house in Charles Street,
at number twenty one
is no longer standing
every brick has gone.

It was the place where I was born
my brother and sister too,
It was only small, and not tall
and rooms were very few.

But it was home with a large coal fire,
for everyone to see
I used to sit and count the flames
upon my mother's knee.

It had a little cellar
that was underneath the stairs.
Where I would play with coal and paper
and pretend to sell my wares.

When winter nights were growing near,
our mum would say 'now don't you fear'.
We'd peg a rug to pass the time,
or we would listen to Harry Lime.
  Louisa Roe

Louisa Roe was born in Ashton-Under-Lyne in 1943. She
writes poetry and short stories for children, one of her
poems being published in Australia. Enjoys writing about the
past.

Why?

Sitting in a room, the four walls close in on you
You've got no money, what you gonna do?
You look all around you - just an empty shell
your existence is just hell.
You search through the papers but to no avail
job after job you search, all have wrong detail
you wish you'd stayed on to achieve
but now it's too late, now you must grieve
You pace the room to and fro
'There must be something I can do'
You haven't washed, you haven't eaten
your clothes look dirty and beaten
you sit down - hands fidgeting
you wonder how you're existing
you put your jacket on. Out you go
down to the job centre - there must be something
                                        to show
you came away with the card of hope
if you get the job you know you'll cope
you hope the money you get will better the queue
if it doesn't and you get it, what you gonna do?
It's just like sitting in a room. Walls close in on you.
  Andreas Wilkopp

Andreas Wilkopp was born in Germany in 1962. He has lived in England for around twenty years and hopes one day to become an established poet.

Children's Ward

Three first year students to ward eight came,
Angela, Chris and Vicky were the names.
If only you knew the fear we hid,
Of all those sick and crying kids.

Screams and shouts all around,
When Carl or Jamie want a bedpan found.
John's here again, but he'll be fine
As soon as he's had his 'Factor Nine'.

Fractures, contractures and abdo pain,
Drips going off yet again.
Bedbaths, pre-meds, theatre trolleys too,
Shouts of 'Nurse I want to poo'.

Check the traction, make the beds,
Do the neuro obs on injured heads.
Observations, temperatures galore,
Cleaning the mess up on the floor.

Grandma, aunts, mums and dad,
More relatives than patients we've had.
Jigsaws and lego on the floor,
Sweet little children wanting more.

Amidst all the hustle we wonder how
We've had time to nurse a fevered brow.
The staff at times so few
Have tried to teach us all they knew.

We leave the ward much wiser now,
Thank you staff and take a bow.
For paediatrics we've learned to treat,
Over this hectic but fun nine weeks.
   Christine Gregson

Chris Gregson is a mature student nurse at Blackburn Royal
Infirmary.

The Night

The earth belows takes its rest, for it is the night
Animals scurry along the way keeping out of sight
The moon so high above, casts shadows on the ground
Lots of tiny creatures, unseen do search around
The rustle of the leaves as to the earth they fall
The silence is shattered by a vixens call
An owl flies silently along, his eyes don't miss a thing
All the earth below, he rules it as a king
The silver rays of a harvest moon, cloaks the earth in sheen
Sleeping mortals here below, dream what might have been
   Amy Savage

Amy Savage gets her inspiration from the beauty of the
countryside and the people who live in it. She has lived in
the country for 77 years and believes there is a lot of
beauty to take care of.

God's Hands

God gave us hands to help us,
To do so many things,
We take out hands for granted
But really this is a sin.
They turn the pages of a book
They hold the one's we love
God's hands were gentle as a lamb
They taught us how to pray.

Without our hands
We could not do
The things we want in life
Our hands they pick a flower
They close an open door
To hold a child
Or hold a hand
Of someone we adore.
   G. Stenhouse

Gwendolyne Stenhouse was born in Northampton in 1940.
Poetry has always been a second nature to her and her
ambition is to have her own collection published.

Our World

CFC's
Harmful gas.
Destroying the ozone layer.
Friendly cans,
Recycled paper,
This is our only prayer.
Rubbish,
Pollution,
Rain forests being cut down.
Lead free petrol,
Litter bins,
Might relieve us of this frown.
Nuclear waste,
Acid rain,
Apartheid - another divider.
Save the whale,
Greenpeace,
Are you a survivor?

The World Wildlife Fund,
Save the Seal,
The threat of the bomb
Our world,
Is falling apart
While we all look on.
    Jenny Humphries

Jenny Humphries is eighteen and lives in Gillingham near
Kent. She has been writing poetry for three years and is
happy to see her first published work.

Lost Without a Soul

Couldn't find the track
Lost wandering in the night
Couldn't see the signs
Nearly lost the fight

Kick you when you're down
Throw you in the dirt
Mock you when you're up
Stone you till it hurts.

Running through the jungle
Living in the hell
When it's time to kill
Disregard the smell

Now the path is clear
Sunlight clouds your eyes
Purpose follows reason
Death becomes disguise

Fear the only courage
Pain the mental spur
Drives you to insanity
Sight begins to blur

Close the door forever
Pushed into the hole
A ghost for all eternity
Lost without a soul.
   Paul Gaffney

Paul Gaffney started writing poems ten years ago, though
mainly for pleasure several poems have been published.

The Child of Divorce

No one understood her
No one had time to care
The victim of two people's incompatibility

Left alone with her thoughts.
Once sheltered from life's cruel realities.

Protected, pampered, private school
Then her childhood shattered
Splintered into tiny meaningless pieces.
Lost, she stands against the world
Amanda 'Fit to be loved'
   Amanda Maddox

Amanda Maddox was born in Kent in 1964. She has been
writing poetry since her school days and hopes to publish
more of her work in the future.

Sadness

Sadness is moving
Moving from home
Away from love.

Sadness is loss
Loss from life
Away to death

Sadness is dark
Dark from light
Away not to go.

Sadness is war
War is death
Death is destruction

Sadness is tears
Tears are sad
Sad is sadness.
　Kieran Williams

Keiran Williams was born in Margate in 1976. He now
attends boarding school in Norfolk and this is his first
published work.

Home of Devon

A warmth of welcome comes
To me in Devon's countryside
A green that doth unfold
It's hills, it's hedges cling
For miles into peaceful
Nestling villages
And trees behold a rustling
Shake of wind.
As hills go up and up to
Our tors.
And show us sights we
Always know are there
A love for it we always share
My mind at peace, I do
Not seek an answer to
My find.
Just a line to say
I love it my own
Special way.
　Diana Hexter

Diana Hexter lives in Devon, and spends most of her time working in Genealogy and knitting for charity.

Change

In spring - my heart leapt for you,
In summer the sun shone down,
By autumn the leaves were changing
And in winter we were cold and through
Why do the seasons have to change, and
Why I ask - did you
   Yvonne Rayner

Yvonne Rayner was born in Manchester in 1963, she writes poetry in her spare time and hopes to publish her own collection in the near future.

Untitled

Why is life so cruel
Why do things get worse
From the day that we are born
Till we go out in a hearse
We make so many promises
And believe in them so true
No soon as we start smiling
Something makes us blue
So we pick up all the pieces
And try to start again
But when it seems we're winning
The ending's just the same
There's nothing we can do
To change this wicked life
It's what it's meant to be
The trouble and the strife.
   Russell Maddox

Russel Maddox is 28 years old, was born in Cannock but has settled in Tamworth with his family for whom he wrote this poem. This is hopefully the first of many published pieces.

Untitled

How many funerals must Ireland see
Till it's sons are all gone and it's women just weep
How many funerals must Ireland see
Till it's young generation grow up to be free
Oh Ireland, Oh Ireland what are you about
Your warmth and your beauty are there to be bound.

But the Ireland I see now has changed many ways
Her burden is heavy though her beauty it stays.
I see churchyards growing where they now lay
Her sons are no longer at play,

How many funerals must Ireland see
Till the soldiers have gone and the people agree
How many funerals must Ireland see
Till the love and the warmth are there to be seen.
Oh Ireland, Oh Ireland what are you about
The years pass so quickly, of that there's no doubt

I see the churchyards growing where they now lay
Her sons are no longer, no longer at play.
  Linda Harrington Dallin

Linda Harrington Dallin was born in Lancashire in 1944. She has written many topical poems.

Tom the Climber

I'm a friend of Celina's, so here is a rhyme
It's about what happened when you went for that climb
The last time she saw you, you were looking quite stiff
Well what do you expect when you jump off a cliff

The forthcoming holiday with you made her ever so glad
But her dreams were shattered when she got a ring from
your dad
Telling her of the bad news that he'd heard
That his son had been trying to fly like a bird.

But unfortunately it didn't work out
You had fallen quite badly whilst wandering about
Onto a ledge for the rest of the night
And when rescued the day after you did look a sight

Fort William was where you were taken
You were badly bruised and really shaken
Clannad music was playing in your swollen head
Whilst you were propped up in your hospital bed

When it first happened you were seriously ill
Because of your state you had to stay completely still
So get better soon so you can get out of bed
And if you go up a mountain, don't fall on your head.
    Donna Louisa Caldwell

Donna Louisa Caldwell was born in Manchester in 1967 and
now lives in Todmorden in West Yorkshire. Her main
ambition is to be a successful writer.

The Wind

The wind, she whirls around the trees
Whistling furiously as she spins the leaves
She hath no care
As she runs her windy fingers through
My hair.
Blowing up and around she tears
The things up off the ground
This lady, this mistress of the day and night
Could you be merciful and hear my plight

-56-

Or is it that you just don't care
As you play havoc with my hair
Oh lady wind please go away
And come again some other day.
  Sonya Lysek

Sonya Lysek was born in Burnley in 1956. She spends her time writing poetry and books and hopes to have some of her work published in the near future.

Call of the Aliens

The power of the press, the nasty media,
Can the human race get any greedier?
You own your world and all it contains
It was a grave mistake to give man brains,
Intelligence was given in order to create
But man uses it to unleash more hate,
Destruction and conflict, the end is nigh,
We space travellers can hear you humans cry,
We know you've had enough of war and doom,
Then come to our world, we have plenty of room,
No wars, no armies, we have a life of ease,
No fear of death, do whatever you please,
You're quite welcome to make your homes in our place
We live far away in the depths of space,
Our beautiful planet of colour and light
Everyone lives together in happiness and delight,
You'll have to get used to the way our inhabitants are
'Coz we look nothing like you on our infinite star
We'll help you out, we'll give you a hand,
But you've gotta stop killing what you don't understand.
  Steve Hayes

Steve Hayes is 27 years old and was born in Sheffield. This is his first published work. His poems have been dismissed by some people as unconnected ramblings, read between the lines to see the meaning.

A Cat in Recession

My mistress died or moved away
I never thought I'd be a stray.
The door is bolted, curtains drawn -
Here I sit on my tidy lawn.

It's summer time and I'm quite fat
Thanks to mice and vole and rat.
Crouched in this fast growing grass,
This time of plenty must not pass.

But pass it does and with it prey,
Perhaps I'll eat another day.
October's here and darker nights
Fighting for territorial rights.

With all the comfort that I had
I never felt I'd feel this bad.
Tail like string and constant scratch,
I'm going through a dreadful patch.

I know where I would rather be,
Free of lice and tick and flea.
Curled tight and warm, and full of cream
On eiderdown in endless dream.

Where has she gone? she was so kind,
A better home I'll never find.
Why was I left in such distress?
Perhaps her home was repossessed!
    Elizabeth Meyrick

Elizabeth Meyrick was born in London in 1939 and has lived
in South Wales for 25 years. She hopes to complete a book
on Welsh village life shortly.

Seasons

Now winter's here the cold wind blows
The snow into my eyes
I long for the day when the snow melts away
And the sun reappears in the skies

When spring comes around
We will walk in the park
Listening for sounds
Of the little sky lark.

When the sky is bright blue
And crystal clear
When the swallow appears
Then summer is here

When the leaves start falling
To the ground
Then we know that autumn
Has come around.

We've heard the four seasons
In this rhyme
Now back we must go
To winter time
    Robert McDougall

Robert McDougall was born in Clydebank in 1956. This is
his first published poem and he would like to dedicate it
to his son and daughter.

Fields

O'er the lea so wet in haze
Where the dale so oft in blaize
Wheat, golden in the noonday sun
Spiders silver webs are spun.

Forests radiate it, wooden green,
Meadows explode their dawning sheen
Wander range as a bird on high
With the purple river running by.
   Bob

Barry Charlton is an ex Royal Navy CPO, now living in
Grimsby and driving a taxi.

Lost Dreams

Halls of green and lands unseen, tall ships and ballet
                                            dancers,
Baronets and pirouettes, places and missed chances.
Seas and sand and boats and bands, colours bright and fading.
The night brings all, the dawn the fall, of dreams new
                                            inspirations.

Racing cars, and beams and bars, goals and teams and races.
Winning posts, the final toast, 1st and 2nd places.
The marks are in, champions we win, the joy and cheer
                                            resounding.
As night wears on, the darkness gone, the morn the dream
                                            dissolving.

Choices, changes fear and pain, as mind and body wakens.
Jealously, conflict, confusion and heartache, has life really
                                            been forsaken.
Faraway the world doth sway, reality in its keeping.
Making safe our future day, when we've done with all our
                                            dreaming.
   Jean Bell

Jean Bell was born in Scunthorpe in 1954. She writes short
stories and poems as a hobby and this is the first time she
has submitted anything for publication.

Oh Silver Hair

Oh silver hair and deep sad eyes
your wrinkled brow and heavy sighs
with a broken heart and taunting jeers
I gave to you with endless fears
your lonely days and nights of stress
and worried mind that gives you no rest
were my gifts to you as I said goodbye
when I left you alone - to live or die
I gave you nought but strife and fears
when I left you alone to face the empty years
I gave no embrace, no hope, or cheer
and never once said - I love you - my mother dear
you have no one to love, and no one to care
no ray of hope to say for you a prayer
no one to share your days so blue
or say God Bless You, as a loved one should do
But through all the sad years that we've been apart
I've felt a great pain deep down in my heart
for I'm missing you so my mother dear
so please help me to reach you
through my blindness and fear
stretch out your arms, will me to your side
where I shall cling through all ebbs and tides
I'll open my heart and flush away your tears
and pray God will forgive me for our wasted years
so silver hair abide with me
say for me a prayer that will set me free
to share a new life, for just you and me
where together we shall travel to our true destiny.
   J. Anthony Kelly

Antonio Tonaro, an aged Englishman of seventy, of Italian
stock, seeks, searches and yearns to find the master of
music to give him the necessary lessons that will give to
him, the pleasure of a lifetime's dream to sing in the
shadow of the great Caruso.

The Mountain

Deep purple mountain, so regal and grand
It's silent you are, as in splendour you stand
Not of this earth, aloof and apart
Wonderful treasures lie deep in your heart

Great man that you are, so wise and so old
To you of your troubles, sad men they have told
Your cloak a brown mantle, your crown is of snow
Buds you will shelter from cold winds as they blow

Men, they have climbed you a flag there to place,
You smiled in your wisdom, unbowed in your grace
No man is your master, your shoulders won't bend
You'll live on forever, your time has no end.
  Gordon McDonald

Gordon McDonald was born in Glasgow in 1940 and has lived
in the north of the city all of his life. He writes poems for
a hobby.

Obscurity

I can see you, but I can't
really see you, because today
obscurity has become
a way of life. It's so deceptive.
You hide away from me.
Come out of your shell
show me the beauty you
lock up inside of you
Why, why there is no reason
for you to go on like this
You just go on and on and
life will be finished before
you give in, you say that it
is ingrained in you, it is not
You say your mind plays

tricks on you, it does not
it's just that stubborness
that is built up in you
like the scale on a pot?
Get rid of it
and I will love you.
    Joe McElarney

Joe McElarney lives in Ireland. Innovations, art, poetry,
chess, and engineering take up most of his time. He is at
present doing a City and Guilds course in engineering.

A Summer's Ride

He turns the key, the engine roars
High above the Kestrel soars,
His mind is alert and full of life
For any sign of trouble and strife.

The wind is blowing cool and fresh
He feels a tingling in his flesh,
He checks the speedo, fifty four,
She'll do more, she has before.

Up a gear and throttle back,
This bike of his will never lack,
He feel the heat beneath his feet
A summer's ride cannot be beat.
    Anne Madden

Anne Madden was born in Sheffield in 1968. She is a
housewife with two children and has been writing poetry
since the age of twelve and hopes to have them published
in the future.

The Ancient Mariner and the Albatross

You are the ship, lost at sea
I am the albatross, born to be free
The sea's my friend, she moves me as I fly
As storm sets in, waves run high
Breaking your bows as your sails do sigh.
Spinning round and around you'll go
But I am watching you, you know!
Because I can guide you to the shore
Where adventure roams for ever more
In the still of night, all seems fine
You'll hear my cry and know it's time
For deep and far, I'll take you out
Into the skys I'm on and about
So follow me, I'll lead you through
The rainbow arch, forever true...
   D. J. Avery

D. J. Avery was born in Hitchin in 1961. She has been an artist since childhood and started writing poetry at fifteen.

For What?

Shots ring out in the morning sky
No-one stops to wonder why.
A battle fought for far too long.
And endless feud going on and on.

Death's a word so close to you
Don't think about it, it's a job to do.
An unending cause for which you fight,
As you lay dead on a cold dark night.

No-one cares because it's not them.
No silent prayers for those dead men.
Every day's a war on open streets,
Soldiers blood at children's feet.

And if another is killed to day
Blown up by a bomb from the IRA
Would everyone his praises sing
Would his death mean anything?

And who will have won at the end of the day?
Only politicians have their say.
But for all those men who have met their fate,
A day of peace will come too late.
   A. Godley

Annette Godley was born in Gainsborough, Lincolnshire, in
1968. She hopes this will be the first of many poems
published.

My Photo Album

I sit here all alone
and flick through photographs,
Some that captured sad times
but most of them the laughs.

And even some of you
a smile on every one
Even some of us on holiday
where you and I had fun.

We were just another couple
in love and meant to be
God made us for each other
and this anyone could see.

But then while looking back
I ask my reasons why
Looking back on memories
being lonely makes me cry

I know you're taken care of
and the Lord thy soul does keep
But every lonely morning
I lay there and I weep.

If only we could start again
and a second chance was mine
I'd make sure that while we lived
for you the sun did shine.
    Steven Eastwood

Gold

It reminds me of you
Beautiful to look at,
Precious, rare and powerful
Magical and mysterious,
Treasured but never possessed,
And when you find it
You realise you can never totally own it
For it has a life of it's own,
Remember me by it.
    Gillie

Gillian Lock was born in London in 1958, but has lived in
High Wycombe for thirty years. Has won prizes for her
poetry and would like to dedicate this one to Gary.

Lonely Planet

With your yellow book and copy tapes
You went across Asia to find yourself
Travelling out of season to find life's reason
Looking for your place on this lonely planet.

You hitched down the Kora Koram Highway
Passed through China and took the road to Mandalay
Climbed a volcano three thousand metres high
Even found a lost tribe in North Chang Mia.

From the finger tipped mountains, to the Chocale hills
The Hanging Gardens to the Pancake Mills
You always found a lover, be it Bali or Goa
But just like beaches, they were like any other

You climbed the Golden Staircase to the Moons Gate
Watched the sunrise over your Japanese date
Then sat and watched it set over the roof of the world
And shouted what on earth am I doing here girl?

But finding yourself is like the eighth wonder
It's not the Taj Mahal, or the Great wall
The terraces of rice or Indonesian spice
It's you looking for your place on this lonely planet.
  Colin Pearson

The Devils Image

I am a shadow, I am a sylph
I slip in and out of darkness
I climb to the highest slate
I crawl on the lowest floor
But it's doors I use most of all
I bring misery and pain
Sometimes I bring some gain
I am constantly in mind
It matters not if you are blind
I am the fear of the unknown
Watch out, minds can be blown
Watch the images that are conjured
Nuclear bombs hold no terror
Compared to me, old fella
Old folks I also make my victims
And them that keep it in tins

I am a loner no friend to talk of
You won't see me in company or mob
There's them that follow in and out
Up and down, round about
It's their job all things to know
That's what they've been known to crow
Sometimes in riches I'll be rolling
More often I'm penniless, gauling
You're bound to meet me anywhere
Doing the shopping or in the square
Yet if you should catch me in your eye
You'd walk on, pass me by
You wouldn't give a second look
Because you won't see me as a crook.
    E. Watkin

E. Watkin was born in Barnsley, now living in Penistone. He
retired early in 1982 and joined the Barnsley WEA Writers
Workshop, to write poems and short stories.

Give Me Myself

Pain searing through my head,
Through my mind, my heart.
Blinding anger explodes before my eyes
My passion is out of control,
I can feel nothing
And yet I am feeling everything.
Hopelessness drowns me
I am consumed once more
Sucked into a vortex
I am powerless to escape.

Running, screaming, hurting
My love is an endless merry-go-round
A pattern repeating itself.
Already I know how it will end.
Will these feelings haunt me forever?
Is my sentence to be frustration?

Hell on earth?
Feelings too powerful to explain,
Total blind fury burning up inside
Screaming, tearing
Demanding a saviour who will never come.

And still I am weak.
Already relenting
I shame myself.
Please someone help
Give me strength
Give me power
Give me myself
Again.
   Briony Grilli

Briony Grilli is the General Manager for a network of
employment agencies is East Anglia. Having spent several
years travelling the world, she now spends her free time
writing poetry. short stories and travel articles.

Voting Day

The politicians confuse us
And the media pile it on,
So who are you going to vote for?
Do you really know old son?

The Labour say they're capable
for one more flipping mile
The Tory's answer with a reassuring smile
But it doesn't solve my questions
are the answers new?
It's all up to us poor voters - folks
like me and you.

They think that we're all barmy
And we want to get rich quick
So here's a pin you voters
Come and take your pick.

Now if you want to be blooming happy
And have lots of breaks for tea
How about yours truly
Come on - and vote for me.
  D. M. Rollason

Marge Rollason was born in Birmingham in 1925 and is now
a retired home help.

Tracks

Along this lonely path
Following in the wake of wiser men,
Visions dance a saraband
Ghosts that call with mystic ken
Roads that lead to nowhere
Criss-cross at a rendezvous
Vanishing points to every line
Signs to say each road is true.
Down the dark and unsoiled tracks
Footprints fail to press upon
Many that tread another's steps
Find the prize has long since gone.
Trails upon the other side
Kindle within a curious fear,
Illusory mists that blanket fast
To know what's there is over here
Look upon these phantom streets
In death and glory swallowed
As tracks upon the pilgrims way
The drumbeat your heart followed.
  Mark Anthony Hogan

Mark Anthony Hogan was born in Liverpool in 1965. Now living in Runcorn, he is an unpublished writer of poetry, a novel and a play.

Ecstasy Addiction

If you've ever seen an addict,
shaking like a leaf
and wondered what he's doing,
he's getting impatient, frustrated.

He may have seen the heavenly Kingdom,
and, dragged off of the pearly gates,
by Mr Right and his busy-bodies,
wants to get back.

If he's walked across lands that are
so much better,
What does he want to hang around here for?

But if he offers you something
suggests you get high
on laughter, music, sex or drugs
don't even think about it,
leave well alone.

Because one trip isn't enough,
you'll want to stay for ever
and reach with grasping hands for
that height.
feeling the earth beneath your feet
so low.
    P. Birch

Paul Birch is twenty and lives in Swindon. He writes poetry in his spare time and hopes to publish a collection soon.

Poems

Under a single stone
A footprint, a leaf is found
By faces careless and free

Four quiet eyes
Soak in the air, and pick
Up last years moisture,
And see -

A single stone,
A footprint, a leaf alone
And hear a wind remember
A loveless afternoon.
    Suman Subba

Suman Subba was born in Penang, Malaysia in 1969. Although
Nepalese by birth he has spent most of his life living in
Hong Kong, Brunei and the UK.

Hope

The old year fast has slipped away
with ghosts from past now kept at bay
with recollections bright and cheerful
with memories of sadness and evil
with days of doubts and nights of fears
with times of hope and joy and tears
These days will in this new year's dawn
return, but with no fear forlorn
For we have heard the angel song
which was of old both clear and long
A song of birth and joy and hope
that in our darkness we may know
the light which love did here bestow
to set us free from sin and death
and give each one, new life, new breath.

So in this year but newly born,
Our Lord and Saviour, we adorn
Who bear our pains and many sorrows
and shares forever our tomorrows
offers himself a balm and haven
till we meet with Him in heaven.
So, with strength and hope renewed
we read His word, and heavenly food
we rest in Him, His grace is near
and in His love, which cost Him dear
we find peace and rest eternal
though days on earth of grief be several
But when our journey here is done
the best is yet to be with Thee
oh bright Heavens Son.
   Margaret Macleod

Margaret Macleod has lived on the island of Lewis for
twenty years. She enjoys gardening, swimming and cycling
and writes poetry in her spare time. Several of her poems
have been published.

Overcoats

Sometimes,
The man puts
A poor coat
Over his rich body
To gain sympathy,
But other times
He washes his new car
When he knows
The neighbours are watching.
This man
Has the best house
In his street
But cannot smile,
And is too busy
Planning the next pay rise,

To have time
For those who are
Less fortunate than himself.
I know a vagabond
Who often wears
An overcoat in July,
But he has smiles
Inside his pockets.
  Ray Jon

Ray Jon was born in Essex. He has appeared in numerous poetry magazines and published two collections of poetry, 'In Search of Forever' and 'Plane of Peace'.

A Fairy Dream

A tip toeing through the bracken on a Sunday
morning. I heard a little crackling,
It was not up above in them yonder trees,
Nor was it below in the undergrove
It was in between in the shadOw of an oak.

It was the little folk, dressed in woodland green
With black and buckled shoes and tulip hats
A singing and a dancing around a daisy bed.
It was a cheery sound it went straight to my head

There in the centre, I saw the fairy queen
Upon her toadstool throne, On her head a thorny crown
A table laid with bramble pie and chestnuts brown
A squirrel stood by, looking starry eyed, awaiting
For a peck.

A rabbit sneaked out from under a thatch
And looked very smart with a tray of
Jam tarts. Her majesty said 'Don't tuck in
Until I begin,' then they all joined in.

The snowy dove sent down her love
Just then I slipped on a snail
And hit my head on an old rusty pail
I awoke in my bed was it a dream
Or a fairy tale.
   Duncan Macfarlane

Duncan Macfarlane is a full time student of horticulture.
He was born in Glasgow and has had a couple of his poems
recorded for radio programmes.

The Witch

Three witches sat around the floor
To cast their spell of doom
They drew a magic circle
and chanted to the moon.
The curtains started moving
and the lights were going dim
as the witches cast their evil spell
on poor old Tiny Tim.
He was the poor old gardener
who always lived alone
He didn't like the witches
since they drove him from his home.
They shouted 'Okus Pokus'
and pointed to the sky
Then poor old Tim just flapped his wings
and found that he could fly.
He flew away just like a bird
no one has seen him since
Did the witches banish him from earth
It really makes you think.
   Ruth Long

Ruth Long lives in Boston and has been writing poetry for
family and friends for many years.

A Day

Today I saw a hidden place
Seasons selected of spiritual skies
For beauty spun, it's web unclaimed
the face of a petal, oh so plain.
An acorn fell but no one saw
the mirage, the mirror's, the open door.
The earth on my toes so soft and sincere,
tracing shadows, temptation lay near.
Blowing near to my shoulder the audience of leaves
a threshold of peace making love to the trees.
Fixed ideas watched by reflecting eyes
hollow heads on minds that die.
The twilight of dawn it comes in grey,
the early morning, the brand new day.
   C. Foster

C. Foster was born in Newcastle on Christmas Day 1961.
She now resides in Winchester and dedicates 'A Day' to her
mother Aileen.

Wings

If I had wings to fly.
My dreams would be in the sky
then my heart would jump with glee
for beneath me would be the sea.
The sea would be rough
and the winds would blow
and my wings would touch
the sea below.
But in my heart
I would not care
For Heaven is always there
Heaven would be like a nest
where I could lay my head to rest.
   David Gethin

David Gethin was born in Wales in 1938. He enjoys writing song lyrics and positive poetry.

Nostalgia

What is this we're fighting for?
To help a war torn world to peace,
As we've always done of yore?
To hold the brutal Hun at bay
Till the talkers tell us, 'Cease,
And throw your arms away'?.

I know what I'm fighting for,
When tender hands caress my brow
In dreams, on some far distant shore.
Heart calling heart, though no words spoken,
Saying that mines by separation broken;
Drives me to fresh endeavour, to try by my own small part
War's cruel bonds to sever.

And if attempting I should fall,
Remember this my own:
'Twas not for honour, all;
But way of life and thoughts of home,
Winging to you across the heaving foam.
    James H. S. Fowler

James Fowler served throughout the war in the Royal Navy on the lower deck. He retired in 1972 as a Lieutenant Commander, and has written many poems and some prose.

Old England

What's happened to old England? the lions claws are
                                    withdrawn;
Once we were so proud of her, now she can't even purr.
The chirpy London Cockney too, has moved on and left no
                                    trace,

Their little homes demolished and concrete took their place.
Our sleepy country village with the Smithy too has gone -
Green fields fast disappearing, for roads and blocks of stone.
Gone too, the little grocer at the corner of the street,
Who sold us nearly everything, and neighbours their you'd
                                                          meet.
I'm thankful that I knew England, when she was in her prime
Though it's sad to see what she's become, that others can
                                                         deride.
Look what's happened to my country, once she held her head
                                                       up high,
Nations then loved, feared and respected her, this they can't
                                                     deny -
But now she sleeps, she slumbers long, her children seem
                                                   forgotten,
Our Heritage to strangers given, are we so besotted?
Wake up! You sons and daughters and help to win this fight
Forget your Greed and bend your backs our country's plight
                                                    put right,
The once again she could be great, if we all play our parts
And only then she'll rise again, But we must give our
                                                  hearts.

  Barbara Barrett

Barbara Lilian Barrett, born Custom House, London in 1918.
Her earlier years were spent in a childrens home with her
two sisters, May and Win, lived in Romford, Essex for the
past 58 years.

Redundant,

My job's been took away
By people I don't know
A piece of paper in my hand
It told me I'm to go
Life's hard enough today
But without a job at hand
It wasn't much before today
And now it's not that grand

Redundant what a thing to be
Now a number on a list
The one who took my job away
Didn't know that I exist.
   Clifford Walwyn

Clifford Walwyn was born in 1954 in Birmingham, now living
in Telford and presently unemployed. This is his first poem
ever to be published.

You're Not Alone!

Interruption of peace, invasion of Kuwait
Terror and fear escalate

Disruption of lives, death-threats from Iraq
The fight begins to win livelyhood back,

From 1990 to 1991
Peace talks failed the war is on!

The distinct sound of missiles heard over Baghdad
War turns vicious, feeling turn bad.

Across the desert, countless troops,
Advancing in their chosen groups,

Our hearts go out, to women and men,
To each and everyone of them.

Very few live, thousands die,
Innocent lives taken, why?

Dads, husbands, uncles, cousins and brothers
Sisters, wives, girlfriend's and mothers.

You're not alone while you're out there,
Our thoughts are with you, we all care.

Who is this man Saddam Hussein!
Who caused us so much grief and pain.

Alas! Kuwait is liberated,
Still, in our minds a war of hatred,

Remembered are the troops we lost,
Through rain and shine, hail and frost.

They haven't left us, they're still here,
So don't be sad, or shed a tear.

To all our troops, who rest in peace
One day soon, the war will cease!
   Sharon Loney

Sharon Loney was born in Leicester in 1970. Sharons poems
are normally based on experiences, or conflicts around the
world. This poem is dedicated to the families and the
soldiers who fought in the Gulf war.

Peace and Love

The world would be a better place,
If we slowed down the human rat race,
The material things we all enjoy,
Not the dirty air the rivers that smell
Lets clean up this earth for all to enjoy.
Just as it was when I was a boy.
   Keith Porter

Keith Porter was born in Cirencester in 1939. Now living
in Cheltenham, he hopes to write more poems if there's a
market for them.

A Little Boy and His Mum

A little boy plays in the street
Hoping and praying his father he'll meet,
Day in day out it's always the same
Alone he plays his little games,
Until one day he asks his mum
'Tell me please where daddy has gone,
Is he still working far away
Too far to come home for just one day'?
She pulls him close to her side
Say's with a trembling voice she tries to hide,
'Your daddy he is watching you
so you must grow up good and true'.
The little boy say's to his mum
'I can be good and still have fun,
Last night in bd I heard you cry.
You still love daddy
Mummy so do I'
　　John Cowell

John Cowell has lived in Fleetwood all his life. He was a
skipper and co-owner of the largest inshore trawling fleet
in the port of Fleetwood, until retiring in 1985 after
suffering a stroke.

Religion and Race

Religion and race
The cause of all wars
One god we all share
One god we all created
This world that we live in
The beauty of new life
Our god he created
For us to share, it's beauty
But all bruised and bleeding
Our world that is weeping
Nuclear warfare

Millions starving
Bombs exploding, people falling
People no more
This world that we live in
Racial hatred, why
Conflicting religions
Why do we destroy
The beauty created
One god on his own
Our world that is weeping
We should all be ashamed
There should be no divisions
In religion and race.
   Diane Verran

Diane Verran was born in 1962, now living in Witney, with
her twin sons. She writes poetry in her spare time, this
is her first published poem.

The Landing

All my life I've never believed,
In beings from outer space,
But not so many years ago,
I met one face to face.

It was a dark November evening,
And I well remember the fog,
As I walked along the common,
With Skip my little dog.

It was the noise that seemed to scare me first
And then the reddish flame,
Then suddenly I realised
With this was not a game.

A flying saucer had landed,
Before my very eyes,
I hardly dared believe,
That these things came from the skies

The side screwed open slowly,
I could see it through the fog,
A being came out, a terrible thing,
And it grabbed my little dog.

I couldn't help but panic,
As I turned and ran away,
I loved my little dog,
But I hadn't the nerve to stay.

My little dog was murdered,
The details were quite gory,
And I never saw my Skip again,
But please believe my story
   John James Ramm

John James Ramm was born in South Shields, and is a
retired gas worker, and several of his poems have appeared
in Modern Poets Eighties

Football

Running, jumping, falling down,
Leaping high up off the ground,
Chasing, dodging, shouting out,
Kissing, hugging, arms about.
Dancing, dribbling, heads collide,
Getting kicked on knee or thigh.
Chants with taunting can be heard,
The crowd are giving you the bird.
Tempers raised, elbows out,
Prodding ribs and chest about.
Whistle blowing very hard,
Being shown the yellow card.

Lungs exploding, gasps for air,
Muscles tight, some bruises there,
Soaked in sweat from body heat
Freezing in the winter sleet,
All to chase that leather ball,
To score a goal, and hear the roar.
Victory is to walk on air,
Lose, you feel that gut despair.
No other game can quite compete,
With football, played on pitch, or street.
   Margaret Miller

Margaret Miller was born in Portsmouth. She enjoys writing
and has had some success with her poems in competitions.

Scared

'Nothing scares me' thought the boy on the bike,
as he called his school teacher a silly old dyke,
'Nothing scares me' boasted the boy with the knife,
then he stabbed his best mate without even a fight.

'Nothing scares me' said the girl in black gear,
'if you don't take drugs, you must be a queer',
Nick this - punch that, see how though I can be
'these older folk are just scared, can't you see?'

'Poor things' I think as I sadly pass by
Why oh why won't they - or can't they try,
to see as I see, just how scared they all are,
more so than the older folk, by far.

Scared of conforming, of being the same
as the older generation, who to them seem so tame,
Scared of doing the decent thing
or the scorn of their friends on their own heads they'll
                                       bring.

  Jane Pringle

Jane Pringle, born in Ilmington has lived most of her life in Nuneaton. Writes for pleasure, including short stories for her four year old Granddaughter Natalie. Has never before submitted anything for publication.

A Game of Chess

You and I play chess every day
We don't play to win
We play to live
If we played to win we would
Lose all our friends
You and I play chess every day
We sometimes play to win
We sometimes kick the board flying
And slowly pick up the pieces
You and I play chess every day
Some people have trouble playing
Some can't play
Some are great players
You and I play chess every day
If you're not very good at chess
We could have a game of draughts
We don't play to win
We play to live.
   Colin Farquhar

Colin Farquhar although new to the publishing world, hopes to have a collection published one day, for his baby son, Luke. He has been penning poetry since the early 80's.

The Country Lane

Looking at the sparkling rain drops
Falling oh so tenderly
Life is so false
Time goes so fast
How I long my life to last
I wander past my childhood past

Down winding country lanes
Looking at the fresh green grass
Moist with raindrops
Childhood memories pass me by
The country lane is the one to blame.
  Warren Hughes

Warren Hughes was born in 1962 in Bedfordshire. An ardent
supporter of Leeds United FC, he enjoys classical music,
golf, and walking in the countryside. He now lives in East
Sussex where he writes poems and short stories.

Refugees

'We are the Kurds and we are here to stay,'
I hear their chant from faraway,
They've run away from Saddam Hussein,
The cruel dictator who has gone insane,
They seek refuge in Turkey and in Iran,
They are fleeing in the thousands, from vicious
                                    Saddam.

The brutal dictator, the devious old man,
They plan death for Saddam,
But the scheme backfired.
Now they are dying a thousand or more each day,
There's no help for the Kurds they are dying away.

A little girl stares,
Just look in her eye,
She is pleading for help.
There's no sign of a smile

A baby is screaming.
She is thirsty and tired,
Her mother is crying
There's no hope in her eyes.

Their chant has disappeared,
They are getting weaker each day,
With disease moving swiftly,
The next person waiting to invade.
  Vicky Jones

Vicky Jones is a 15 year old student studying for her
G.C.S.e's at Mynyddbach school in Swansea. This poem was
written as an assignment for her English.

A Maisonette Existence

A maisonette existence is a funny old life
Thrive off self - sufficiency on the edge of a knife
Two in a bed and the little one cried
There's only room for one, luckily my soul has died.

A maisonette existence without an ensuite
Too many people use the sink to wash imaginary feet
Stickle - bricks can create a fantasy inside
Where feet are never discussed between Jeckyl and Hyde.

A maisonette existence where relationships reside
Burning spanish omelette will not stem the tide
Deterioration between two stools is therefore a must
But on a metorphorical giro, it's a maisonette or bust.
  Simon Bond

Simon Bond is the archetypal "could do better" boy of
achievement. Somewhat of a waster, he is, however, a nice
chap who points the finger at both Mark and Amanda for
making this gem possible.

Hideway

My den: a haven,
It's my secret place, my hideaway where
Vanished are the trouble days of school,
In here it's pure play.
Here I escape the taunts of the bully,
She picks on me because I'm small;
But one day I'll change from ugly duckling to swan
Never again to fall.
It's a safe place but a cold place,
But I'm away from harm,
It's somewhere where my childish games
Aren't shattered and torn
By parents who don't understand.

I'm young and acclaimed innocent
By the laws of this land.

My den is set in woods near home,
And is made from branches and leaves,
It's out of sight of any eye
And out of my parents reach.
The games I play are very simple:
Nothing like those in school,
The games are just for one
Where I don't end up the fool.
I've set aside my own little world
Which I return to every day,
Where parents and bullies don't exist
In my secret hideaway.
   Gerald Chavezy Wall

Gerald Wall has been a poet for six years. For the past
year he has been writing childrens books, six in all, which
he hopes to have published.

Dream Street

A starry sky is full of dreams
and on the streets below
No one feels my loneliness
And no one wants to know
I close my eyes and picturise
The people I could meet
When I take another walk
down on dream street
Dream street, there's no worries
No one's too slow and no one hurries
there's no illness and no war
there's been no-where like this before
You'll meet who you want to meet
down on dream street
a place where everyone is free
a smile on every face
Where everyone's included
and no ones out of place
Dream street theres no worries
No one's too slow and no one hurries
You'll be what you want to be
a film star or an attorney
You'll meet who you want to meet
Down on dream street
But when the nighttime turns to day
We have to put our dreams away
Go back to need and war and pain
but then tonight I'll go again
I meet who I want to meet
Down on dream street.
   Nicky Speakman

Nicky Speakman is 20 and lives in Leeds, She loves art and
poetry. Writing a poem is like a release, it's like sharing
your feelings with a friend 'Life Inspires Me'!

Temporary Cochise

I sit here in my wheelchair watching the TV screen,
I'm trapped within these four walls, but I'm running in my
                                              dreams.
I'm every handsome hero, each film brings new release,
A knight in shining armour, a temporary cochise.

Four legs good, two legs bad, was written by someone,
Well two legs may not mean much, but it's two better than
                                              none.
I'm Robin Hood on two wheels, I catch the dreams I please.
Saddle up this iron horse, I'm a temporary cochise.
I've won the war a thousand times and shot criminals dead,
I may be much restrained here,
I race to the Antarctic, climb Everest with ease,
Sailing on the Spanish main, a temporary cochise.
    Thomas A Rattray

Thomas A Rattray is a Scotsman now living in Cumbria,
twenty-nine years old, he has written over one thousand
poems, songs and short stories since 1982, but has only
recently submitted work for publication.

Love Tryst

Oh take me to the Isle of Love
Where mermaids play in turquoise pools
And nymphs with wonders of delight
Call no man fool -
And on a lily bed I'll lie
To taste the fruit and golden wine
A paradise of constant love
Green Isle of mine -
Then bring to me a maiden fair
Of guarded wit - of pure delight
And we will play sweet natures game

All through the night -
Flame of passion join us both
In loves stupor softly sway
Woman - fallen as a leaf
Awaken with the day.
   Christopher Wayne

Christopher Wayne - Born is Seaham County Durham has
lived in the West country for many years, his ambition to
write and have published his own collection of 'Everlasting
Verse' for all ages.

Pollution

People drop litter all over the sand.
They have little respect and just ruin our land
Litter makes everything seem so untidy
Without a doubt our world is unsightly
People don't care where they leave it to lay
They don't even try to throw it away.

People use aerosols every single day
Roll-on deodorants are better than spray
The beaches are so polluted and bad
Depression is rife and people feel sad.
Pollution has ruined our world and our land
The officials say swimming may soon be banned.

My message to all before it's too late
Think of your environment and save your fate
   Rebecca Court

Rebecca Court aged fouteen was born in Chatham, she
attends Christchurch High School. Her hobbies are reading
and writing poetry.

Back Alley

The cobblestones grim,
The poverty rife,
Little mean cots
What a life
For folk to live,
Barefoot kids, shaven heads,
Ringworm, rickets and all the rest,
Pale wan faces among the filth,
Mothers old before their best,
Deliver babes, lay out the dead,
Take in washing, scrub, scrub, scrub,
Fingers deformed by the dolly tub,
Drunken father, part of lifes dross
No work, but money for the pub,
Who cares if kids have got no shoes
Street corner fights, pitch and toss,
Coppers come, always in two's
Fetch the priest, they'll listen to him,
Scared to death of the Reverend Flynn,
Usually as drunk as them.
Little girl dies, where does she lie
Take off a door, lie her there
Under the window, in the little hovel.
Life goes on around her, poor little devil,
Ten days to bury her, never forget the smell.
No money to spare, then war comes, well,
Plenty of money for guns and hell.
      Roy Whitfield

Roy Whitfield born in the shadow of the belching, soot laden
bottle ovens of the pottery factories, in the depression
years of the 1920's. Hopes to publish, poems and short
stories of that era.

Solitude

Gather from these solitary moments peace,
And from every seconds quietude distil
Healing essence for your crowd - betrampled soul
True sweet spiken and upon its wounds to spill.
Here, alone, there is no longer need to veil
Inmost secret thoughts from prying public gaze
Here are none to wonder at this self revealed.
Heart unsheathe yourself, deep thoughts unfold; for days
Privacy may not return - you cherished dreams
From their tedious daytime bondage now release -
Treasure in your soul this precious quietude
Gather from these solitary moments, peace
   Mary Hunter

Mary Hunter is a retired Librarian who lives in Leeds, she
has just finished a novel which she hopes will be published
and is at present writing a second one.

Untitled

Love is a thing that never is fair
One day you're down then up in the air
Emotions come in and they play their part
Allowing your head to by ruled by your heart
Fight as you will you never can win
So why keep on struggling just slowly give in.
   Terry Moult

Terry Moult, 43 years young, happily unemployed, and
divorced with 3 teenage children. Two poems have been
published in the freezer magazine. He has a great sense of
humour, enjoys taxing his brain with quizzes.

The World

The world is set on evil deeds.
To fight and kill each country bleeds.
What good who wins -
No peace they find,
When wicked ways beset mankind.
There's so much joy can make life good
In living as a brotherhood.
Our children must not grow and hate,
But turn around, it's not too late.
For love and kindness are the way
To brighten up each others day.
For uphill climbs no skills they lack
To make them vow
No turning back.
    Merna Stalker

Merna Stalker recently started writing poems; mainly about
people, and the world of today. She likes to help with
disabled and elderly people, who can give alot of joy.

To My Husband

When you said you loved me,
I thought your words were true,
When you said you needed me,
I knew I needed you.

The day that we got married,
Was the best day of my life,
I couldn't remember a single day,
Before I was your wife.

The years have passed by now,
and, all I can do is cry,
I've read again your letter,
The one that said 'goodbye'.

My happy world is shattered,
I cannot feel my heart,
Have you really gone for good.
Will we always be apart?.
　　Lee Woollett

Lee Woollett lives in Coventry with her three children.
'To my Husband' was her first poem and because it was
published it will not be her last.

Nearly a Banquet

Meddlesome crows perched on a birch October afternoon
Keep their distance from the tiller working late
Noise of machinery cutting across the field
All members of this bird family
Eagerly await the appearance of the earthworm

The flower looked splendid; a single delight
Where sycamore and oak stand boldly
You could just see the old mill in the distance
Once so full of industry in a nearby field
Sails too rotten; flaked and cracked paint

A redundant machine that gave
All movement halted on a bleak Autumn day.
　　William Cummings

Bill Cummings lives in Walsall and has interests in poetry,
music and literature.

A Poem for You

Please accept this poem
as a gift from me to you
I wrote it on a rainy day
when you were feeling blue
I've worked so long and hard

to make the damn thing rhyme
but the way people look at it
you'd think it was a crime
So I hope it makes you happy
and stops you from feeling blue
because after all is said and done
I only wrote the damn thing for you.
    G. Blakemore

Graham Blakemore was born and still lives in Bilston in the
West Midlands. He is a full time writer of songs, poetry
and childrens books. Many of his songs have been published
and promoted in the USA and Europe.

Why

I watched a small child
All bent and lame
I say dear God why
It seems such a shame.

I watch the heavens
All starry and bright
I say dear God why
Such a beautiful sight

I watch a blind man
Feeling his way
I say dear God why
Such a penance to pay

I've seen some good things
And some quite obscene
I ask dear God why
What does it all mean

What is the pattern
We're all meant to see
And say dear God why
Please show it to me.
   Joan Walker

Joan Walker lives in retirement with her husband, numerous
goldfish, numerous plants and she enjoys making white wine.

Without You

As the sun hides behind the mountains
And the moon acends the sky
I'm lying here without you
And I keep asking myself why

The silence here is deafening
My body's numb all around
I keep waiting for you to call me
But the phone never makes a sound

I keep thinking of the questions
But the answer's never clear
I keep dreaming that one day
Again I'll find you here

But dreaming's all I've got now
And I hope one day I'll find
That I'll wake up one morning
Without you on my mind
   Wendy Handyside

Wendy Handyside was born in 1968, in Amble,
Northumberland. She moved to Margate in 1991 and hopes
to get more of her work published in the near future.

The Fields of Terror

The rabbit sat on the grassy verge,
Watching her territory disappear from sight,
Generations of wildlife had roamed the fields,
But Orton and Stanground,
Stanground and the city,
And eastern industry must connect,
The fields we must forget.

Man and machine siezed the land,
Without the consent of the wildlife,
They began to turn dwellings so natural into something
Called a parkway,
Man and machine would roar past at amazing speed,
Wildlife! take heed of advice,
Keep away from man's creations.

Away in distance,
Acute little ears poised,
Noise rumbled through the air,
The scene of Queensgate stood so tall,
Cars rushed along the road,
Crushing as they went,
Just to see the complex so grand.

The rabbit sat beneath a beam of Peterborough light,
Looking left and right,
Running! running and heart thumping like a beating drum,
But man and machine are in such a hurry,
The drum beats out of time and stops so suddenly, ·
The parkway of heaven claims a new recruit.
   Amanda Hayward

Amanda Hayward was born in Peterborough in 1971 and
works as a word processor operator. She has cerebral palsy
and is currently writing her autobiography which describes
her disability and her life in a wheelchair.

Fire

I am a flame
All flickering and bright
I keep you warm
Both day and night
Sometimes I get angry
And devour your house
Other times I am quiet as a mouse
You may feed me
With gas, coal or wood
But treat me with care
You always should
When out on a picnic
Take extra care
Should I play with the wind
Then beware!
  Melanie Dudman Millbank

Melanie Dawn Dudman Millbank was born in London 1964,
now residing at Harlow in Essex. Her hobbies include reading,
crosswords and writing poetry, her ambition is to have her
works published and recognised.

Waiting

I wait for a call
The postman to ring,
A boy on a bike
Lovely flowers to bring
I try to read a book
When I go to my bed
But my heart want's to cry
With tears left unshed
You have been away so long

I wrote to you my dear
The days pass so quick
But the nights leave a fear
Has anything happened to you dear friend?
Perhaps love did not start, but what is the end.
  Kathlyn M Bamforth

Kathlyn M Bamforth, widow, born in Peterborough, and a
former dancing teacher, who now lives in Harrogate, has a
family of four and enjoys reading, writing and humour.

Wasted Lives

Turn on the TV, another man dead
The newsreader says he was shot in the head
'How awful' we say, 'what a terrible crime'
A few minutes later, it's gone from our minds,
Don't we realise that man whoever he be
Was a real human being, like you and like me
He once was a child with wishes and dreams
Now he's lying alone in a cold, bloody stream,
How many have died since the troubles began?
How many lives wrecked by the cold hand of man?
How many poor children are left with no dad?
How many wives mourn for the life they once had?
Dear old Ireland, how it must break her poor heart,
To see how we're tearing each other apart
How much blood must be spilled on her lovely green shore
Before we all realise that life should mean more.
May God bless our small island, this beautiful land,
May there soon came a day, when we stand hand in hand
Let's be proud of our country, of the Emerald fame.
Let peace be our motto and love be our aim.
  Sally Clarke

Sally Clarke is a 35 year old housewife. She has had quite
a few poems published in local newspapers. She writes poems
and songs lyrics and her ambition is to have a book of
poems published eventually.

Death

Death will come to those who wait
but so many people get in such a state
but Jesus is always there
to guide them to heaven with so much care

Death is a saddened thing
all it does is hurt so much
but up above Jesus is always there
to give them His love and also His care

Death is not what it seems
there's always someone there
Someone to guide them and hold their hand
Up above the peaceful land

Jesus will love her just as much as me
I worshipped her, her whole life long
I still do now, although she's gone
now Jesus has taken my wife so dear
But in my heart my wife is near.

The clouds above so very white
there is Jesus with His light
His light to heaven, to heaven above
above His clouds, his clouds of love.

Heaven is a peaceful land
with angels all around
but my dear wife has sadly gone
Jesus has taken her with His love so strong.

We hear the angels talking
talking softly in the clouds
their gentle words of comfort
they echo all around.

So guide her ever onwards

to our heaven up above
and take along there with you all
my undying love.
   Julie Dawn Edwards

Julie Edwards born in 1964, spends her time writing and
drawing. She has completed one book of poems and although
only just started in the drawing department hopes to
illustrate a book she is working on with her husband.

The Long Road

Our inhibitions tell us, all cannot be lost
And senses of direction point the way
Frequent twists in narrow lanes keep winding
To open up new roads, avoiding the delay
Eyes are closed to all the unseen dangers
And obstacles are set along the paths
Encircling trees with branches rough and spiney
Do swing and sway at life's dire aftermaths
Watery sunrays filter through the forests
To dazzle mans meagre power of brain
Making senses weaker, no feeling any more
Where does he profit, is there any gain
Shapes and shadows lurk there in life's doorway
Grow long or short as passing daylight fades
Comes the night and visions seem to leave us
And so our eyes are locked behind caged shades
But soon the dawn of sanity will greet us
To draw apart the curtain of unknown
And set the stage for all our human traumas
And try to act, devoid of feelings shown
Little times is left for us to ponder
Then seek the straightest road that we can find
As on through weary years our footsteps take us
Not looking back to see what's left behind.
   Amy Potton

Amy Potton has written poems for the B.B.C. was judged by Michael Aspel and his wife, Elisabeth in a poetry competition and was judged runner up. The said poem is now at Sussex University.

Children of the Weak

Monday's child is the ever winding cog.
Although says plenty, and loud enough to wake the dead,
he says nothing.
Deaf ears hear silence, but he continues, in the vain hope
that some day they will listen.

Tuesday's child is evil. Hands clasped tightly around the
drowning goldfish, they gently and sadistically squeeze.
He smiles, says nothing, then secretly beckons the cat.

Wednesday's child sits alone, her plaitted hair in ribbons,
herself in a pink Sunday dress. She does not speak,
she does not play. In many ways she is no longer a child,
just a puppet on a string.

Thursday's child is not afraid. Up trees, down drains,
anywhere and everywhere. Bruises mean nothing to him,
simply stripes upon his sleeve.

Friday's child is educated, stands tall in his blazer,
and pronounces each and every word precisely.
You smile, even though you despise him, and hope that the
scythe you now hold in your hand, may one day cut him
down.

Saturday's child is rarely seen. Shy, he hides behind the
oak tree he calls father. Dad looks down, shakes his head
woefully, and carries on talking to the unknown visitor.

Pity Sunday's child, for she is leaving, too old to live.
Slipping away she looks back. She is gone, but not forgotten.
　John Murray

John Murray is an A-level student studying English literature.
He was born in 1974 and is currently living in Heywood.

I Never Saw You Vincent
(but you speak to me)

I never saw you Vincent,
but your life was so very sad.
Your paintings are all you had,
I was born long after you had gone,
I like to read your books,
about the story of your life.
Why you took your life and wanted to die,
you do not belong to this world now,
but to Gods heaven in the sky
Oh Vincent why did you die?
You suffered for so long,
but your paintings still live on,
for now you paint for angels,
and God is standing by,
he watched you paint the
Sunflowers, you made them
stand up tall.
My favourite is your Two Boots,
that hang upon my wall,
all your paintings tell a
story of your life of misery,
I never saw you Vincent,
but your paintings speak to me.
Your Starry Nights and the Birds Nest too,
the Reaper in the Field,
and the Sunflowers too.
They hang on my wall,
and speak out for you,
Oh Vincent why did you take your life?
　　Maureen Ginnelly

Maureen Ginnelly was born in Dewsbury in 1952. Her hobbies are poetry and art. She wishes to write more poems about Vincent Van Gogh in the future and have them published.

What is a Man?

What is a man without a woman
but a sum of his unequal parts.

his chest so taut and proud
that would beat with rage and thumping anger
that would fight to defend a country or a woman
but which would cave and crumble for the loss of a woman
which would cry and ache so painfully
and yearn and die for the love of a woman.

his arms so strong and powerful
that could force their presence on unwanted souls
that could carry death itself to the hearts of others
but which would wrap around and hold a love so tight
which would protect that love, a woman
from the world so loud and so bright.

his hands so warm and solid
that could hold and squeeze life from this very planet
that could wage destruction through sword and pen
but which would touch so gently a woman's heart
which would trace so sweetly future memories
down a womans face.

What is a man without a woman?
But a shadow of his former self.
   Paul Andrew Vernon

Paul Vernon is 29, a Devonian, he now lives in Edinburgh. He has never had a poem published before but hopes this won't be the last.

To an Unknown Soldier

To an unknown soldier were the words
Upon the simple wooden cross
Lying in a land so far away
He thought he would return one day.

When war was done and peace returned
And people there once more were free
Then he could go home again
The victory won his country served.

I wonder what he would have thought
Had he known the battle bravely fought
Was for him to come to nought
Even his name in vain they sought.

He was no more than just eighteen
When he marched away, so proud
His boots were polished, buttons bright
So upright in his uniform.

His parents waved a fond farewell
Little knowing that it was their last
Mother holding back her tears
Father saying 'Don't worry mum, he'll be back.'

Now he's just a faded photograph
In pride of place upon the mantleshelf
His parents memories hold fast
Onto the image they saw last.

The once proud boy now lying there
Another symbol of man's futility
When will they ever learn
The meaning of humanity.
  Michael Spencer Thornhill

Michael Spencer Thornhill was born in 1939, he lives in Barrow-in-Furness, Cumbria, and his hobbies are writing poetry, articles and short stories.

Thinking Of...

Thinking of,
Deaths of people before their time,
How are we to know who's next in line,
And we decide about the trivial things to whine,
Unrealising.

Masses starved by famines hand,
Poverty sweeps throughout the land,
While we obey God's strange command,
Accepting.

Countries in conflict start a war,
Millions of innocent fall to the floor,
Is this what we're on this earth for,
Suffering?

Tragedies happen from day to day,
Earthquakes force houses into states of decay,
Is the world really meant to be this way,
Destroying?

Hundreds die while intent on having fun,
Watching football matches and travelling for some sun,
To help these people, what could have been done?
Everything.

Heads of state confer for fighting to cease,
All we ask for is worldwide peace,
But the troubles still continue to increase,
Neverending.

People are still judged by the colour of their skin,
When being the wrong colour is seen as a sin,
Will the narrow-minded ever give in,
Relenting?

Rainforests continue to be destroyed,
Just to keep paper makers employed,
And pollution protesters still get annoyed,
Persevering.

Products on unknowing beasts are tested,
Crime rates are growing so more get arrested,
And increasing additives have to be digested,
Poisoning?

Preserving ozone layers without success,
Green fields and open spaces become less and less,
What's being done about our world in this mess?
Nothing,
Anything?
Hoping.
  Emma Holloway

Emma Holloway is a twenty year old student from Lincoln.
She is in the final year of an American studies and history
degree at Lancashire Polytechnic, Preston.

The Lone Pine

Lonely pine on craggy crest,
Spreading shade for nobody,
Separated from the rest,
Of your coniferous family.

Coarse, gnarled roots so thick and strong,
Grappling with your rocky shelf,
Seeking water, growing long,
To secure your defiant self.

Ripe cones fallen on barren ground,
Shrivelling soon in sun's harsh light,
Wafer like seeds scattering around,
Tossed in the air in a frenzied flight.

Bent by wind and lashed by rain,
Proudly stand, a landmark still,
Solitary in your cold domain,
In safety, from the papers mill.
   Jennifer Wells

Jennifer Wells took early retirement from her post as a
Home Economics teacher in London. She spends her time
between Spain and England. She has only just started to
write poetry.

Dirty Old Town

I wish it was more than just a dream,
To sit down by a babbling stream.
How I long to walk through fields so green,
To smell the country air so crisp and clean.

All I want to do is leave this town,
For all it does is make me feel down,
Everywhere I turn nothing but concrete and brick,
This town really does make me feel sick.

I feel like a rat, trapped in a cage,
Is it any wonder I fly into a rage,
A horrible town so dirty and grey,
There's not even a safe place for children to play.

Dark dirty alleyways strewn with litter,
Even in other towns it's not much better,
Dirty old town your definitely not for me,
You even pump sewage into the sea.

The last bit of land, sold off for development,
You won't be happy until all the land is covered in cement,
Dirty old town, that's the final straw,
I don't think I can take anymore.
    Tom Bell

Tom Bell is a retired gardener who has only recently taken
up writing poetry but finds it enjoyable.

The Deluge

Quick, it's raining, quick open the door.
Let it surround me. Let it pour.
Refreshing me with it's droplets
indulging in the stinging wetness
blinding me with it's force.
Just let it take it's course,
and when the skies are clear again
I'll still have the memories
of that intimate moment with the rain.
Drenched to the skin
I felt a great happiness within,
None the worse for indulging with the fickle outbursts
so whenever it rains, quickly open the door,
Let it surround me. Let it pour.
    Marsha Hall

Joan Beresford was born in Barrow-in-Furness. She finds
writing poetry in all spheres fulfilling, and obliges friends
with Christmas and birthday verses, often under the pen
name of Marsha Hall.

Streetlife

He rises from an alley dark, the rats around him feed
A meal and a nice hot drink he needs to stop this aching
                                                        greed
He slithers up onto his feet, shoes no tread, well worn

Wipes his nose upon his sleeve, his mouth lets out a yawn
His matted hair, he doesn't care, his teeth so black and
                                                     rotten
A crumpled photo next to his heart, memories not forgotten
He wipes away the gathering sleep from the corner of his
                                                     eye
Stares at the busy market street, life quickly passes by
He strolls along an empty path, slowly reminiscing
All the love and care he had, all the joy and kissing
The thought of such a happy past, brings him close to tears
No more hope, no more faith, living without no fears
No-one to give and accept return, even in goodwill
No more wasting peoples time with application forms to fill
Just your life to live alone, memories share just part
No one to take everything you have, except your empty
                                                     heart.

   B.S.

Peter George Marr, alias B.S. was born in Sunderland in
1964. Busy writing a story in verse of his days in the Royal
Navy. This is his first attempt at getting his work
published.

That's Life

Alone we come, alone we go,
From this world of toil and woe.
Should our suffering be in vain,
Lest we come around again.
Struggle and strife are part of life,
All it's undoing and pain.
If you do not learn anything in this life,
Then return you will, the same.
Sadness and heartache are our lot.
Change it if you may,
Morsels of happiness are what you get.
That's your reward and pay.
Learn from your sorrow,
Learn from your strife,

And what you learn will tell
That's life,
The way can be lonely,
United we may be,
This journey that we must take,
Him, you and me.
So lift up your load and carry,
And walk on straight and tall,
Don't be despondent or worry,
To hell with it all.
   Sylvia Lewis

Sylvia Lewis is a funeral receptionist living in London. She hopes to publish a first collection shortly.

Dangerous Love

Expression for a purpose
Portrayal of the love
Proving signs in physicality
Masculinity - femininity
Worthy acceptability.
I've never felt so strong
Save in anger
Both are might
So include right
My widest definition
And my strictest
They make the man sublime
Holy laic code
It must be why
That I see I
Sexual as God-like
(or as near as I'll be on somebody else's earth)
That must be why
The less than perfect species
Doing it as do I
Or just the thought
Makes me cringe, my faeces
   Michael Bates

Michael Bates was born in 1957. He has lived in the Medway towns since the age of four. This is his first published piece which he hopes will be the inspiration for more.

Debut

So long a break
And here again
More water's flowed
Than ink from pen.

A different man
And hard as nails
Emerges now
To kick the bails.

For rules are blurred
The game has changed,
The comfy life
Is rearranged.

Be bold, confront
Life's ghost's. Be brash
What matters brain
In headlong dash?

The scene is brief
The script unclear
Enter the hero
Exit the fear.
 David J. Ayres

David J. Ayres is a teacher of modern language, a qualified pilot and a blues guitarist. His first novel ' A Minor Relationship,' is a finalist for this year's Lichfield Literary prize.

The Legend of the Ninth Legion

A Roman Eagle proudly led
The legionaires who marched ahead
Helmets gleaming, heads held high
Prepared to conquer or to die.

Where did that mighty army go
Whilst seeking for their tribesmen foe
Rebel against their harsh regime
Desert their fearsome war machine?.

Perhaps their fate was all too plain
The ninth were ambushed, most were slain
But proof of this was never found
No dead nor weapons strewn around.

Were all destroyed by act of God
Tempest, earthquake, raging flood?
This symbol of the Roman race
Just vanished without any trace.

Some say at night when laying abed
They hear a phantom army led
By drum and distant trumpet call
Marching ever on to Hadrian's Wall.

Perhaps someone may find a gleam
'Neath waters of some borders stream
A tarnished eagle, symbol dread
Of that mighty empire, long since dead.
  Ronald Hann

Ronald Hann was born in Deal, but has lived in Prestonpans,
Scotland for fifty years. A retired local government officer,
he writes short stories and poetry as a hobby.

Bodybags

Those things are black as night still, quiet unseen.
In a dusty foreign land far away from familiar military
shores.
Naked flesh, red skin, fallen comrade a husband no more.
Two figures stand like giants
carrying this fallen warrior to dark restful black place,
That hulk is placed to its so called eternal peace or rest.
The silent pale face is closed off
from all atmosphere the silver finally flies up
the body is in it's cold placing.
The black entity taken like many
to a flying eagle back to a continental sky
these men don't know of
and never will see in their own eye.
The eagle flies, lands to it's familiar perch
the black hulks taken by men.
A questioning voice a light flash not seen here
a rare thing indeed.
The great men in Whitehall walk with honest expressions and
no sounds made against a questioning eye.
All is quiet on English streets no person catches an eye or
raises an opposing view all unknown and Whitehall requires
them to do.
   James Durnion

James Durnion ia a poet from Cleveland, 'Bodybags' he says
is influenced by the poetry of Jim Morrison as well as a
Morrisonesque version of 'Romeo and Juliet', which has yet
to be published.

Armistice

Remembrance for another year
Product of a mother's fear,
They waved their sons a fond goodbye,
Knowing within that they would die.

They fought for country, freedom to live
High price to pay, a life to give
Two minutes' silence, think of the past
Of men whilst fighting - breathed their last.
    Jean Boon

Jean Boon has two young children and her 'precious' spare
time is dedicated to writing poetry and short stories.

Untitled

I read the script
and the script said:
hold tight, stay right
follow the light to the
top of the telepath
where the spheres play their song
of beautiful silence
to all those of pure heart.
When ego dies
the small man flies
to share wine with the angels
and speak of the beautiful
simplicity of life,
Realise
Real-eyes see through this world.
All this truth, if you believe it,
But the truth is beyond belief.
To belly Eve is to deny your true home
now travel, brother,
and find your sister
for only with her
can nature wrap you once again,
in her gentle womb.
Now is our time to be,
From the very beginning we were.
Remember curiosity?
    David Lee Martin

Lee Martin is 19, going on 20, he lives in Brighton and spends most of his time dreaming, writing, and wishing. He hopes to find the love he knows is real.

Unwanted Child

Can you feel me mammy
inside of you,
I'm feeling alright
So comfortable too.

I cannot move, I cannot talk
I cannot see
I'm in the dark.

But I can think,
and I know the day,
I hear them mammy
what they say.

'There is no chance,
there's nothing we can do,
to have it removed is best
for you'.

What do they mean,
take it away,
Do they mean me mammy
is that what they say.

What are they doing,
I wish I could see,
make them stop mammy,
they're hurting me.

They're coming mammy,
proceeding with caution,
I understand now,
your to have an abortion.

They've got me now,
I'm going away,
I love you mammy,
but they wont let me stay.
   Charisse Jon Brown

Charisse Brown lives in Wiltshire though she was born in the
North East of England. This poem is one of many, which
she has enjoyed writing.

Ghostly Bride

I'll close my eyes and think of you,
and the way you curl your hair,
your laugh rings out so loud and clear,
I know that you are near,
I smell the rose I gave you,
on our first anniversary,
The colour of your wedding dress,
The pale lace and the ivory,
Your satin slippers so dainty,
you were my dream, so real.
Then I remembered you died last spring,
and I'm still wearing your wedding ring,
the fever came, you went your way,
to live with God, for the rest of your days.
But my darling you are the most,
my loving, laughing friendly ghost.
We'll be together one day soon,
until then I'll think with pride,
of my loving, laughing ghostly bride,
to me there cannot be another,
who'll fill my heart and be a mother.
To our darling little girl,
who's hair will curl,
as she twists and twirls on our second,
anniversary, her lovely smile,
the same as yours.
Pink rosy cheeks, not a flaw,

so goodbye my darling friendly ghost.
I'll open my eyes now.
Then I will gently slip away,
for another day.
   Pat Evans

Pat Evans was born in Hudswell in 1931. She married Jim
in 1954 and has had four children. She has lived in
Hartlepool for the past 30 years.

Mrs Pickin's Chicken

Mrs Pickin bought a chicken
And took it home for tea.
She wrapped it in foil
Put the spuds on to boil
And sat down with a cup of tea.
While she was sitting
Out jumped the chicken
And said 'Please don't eat me,
Have some bananas
Or even sultanas
But please, just set me free'.
A surprised Mrs Pickin
Looked down at the chicken
And said 'How can this be?
This must be a trick
Get back in there quick,
You can't make a fool out of me
But the chicken just laughed
And ran off down the path
And although this was funny to see,
Poor Mrs Pickin
Didn't have chicken,
She had sausage instead for her tea.
   Janette Sibley

Janette Sibley is an automotive production worker. She was born and is living in Stoke-on-Trent. She mainly writes poems about her family, but also writes a humorous selection for her three children and their friends.

Of War

How came I to be in this place,
This hell where I was sent,
Perdition now, I unwillingly face,
With my death so imminent.

Above, around me, all I see,
Are faces torn with compunction.
I desperately seek for a chance to flee,
This cursed, wanton destruction.

My shattered mind, cracked with the strain,
Cries, 'Stop, no more, no more'.
My body weary, wracked with pain,
For peace I beg, implore.

I know I shall die, I know not how,
My fate is in His hands,
But Lord, my God, if you're with me now,
Don't take me here, in this foul land.
    Deena Tallow

Deena Tallow is 35. At the moment, she is studing for her A'levels in English language and literature. She hopes to one day compile a book of short stories, and satirical sketches.

Opportunity

So fast, I cannot see.
Is it that my net is too small
or my arms too slow?

The grind of the years can be heard
above the cries of wise old people.
And with each passing day I grow older.
Yet like a kite to the wind, I soar.

Rising above the continual whispers of
silver haired men and bespectacled old ladies.
Could they be blinded by their years?
Unable to see the glittering amidst crystal waters?
Or could my eyes be searching the puddle for an ocean?

Sometimes answers are hard to find, but my net will last.
Brushing amongst possibilty like a breeze across the grass.
    Mark Newbery

Mark Newbery was born on the Isle of Wight in 1973.   He
has spent the last two years writing poetry and short stories,
and is currently working on his first screenplay.

Whispering Winds

Oh, whispering winds - Oh, wispering winds
Why do you return to haunt my dreams -
Thinking of days of yesteryear -
When we were young and had not a care -
I want to hold out my hand
To touch friends of bygone days
Do they cast thoughts back
Sometimes and think of me
When we were in our prime -
Do they think, work and play
Times we spent, when we were young -
Do they think of me, as a friend

As I hope or just indifferent
Perhaps a joke -
Are they still amongst us - or
Gone to a better land -
Oh, whispering winds, winds -
Whispering winds - I
Wish I knew, then
I would understand -
The thoughts, that goes
Prancing around my head -
Of people that I knew - so
Long ago, away out in the past
Whispering winds - just
Still my mind -
That the dreams that haunt me
From the past - so I can rest
Then the whispering winds
Would blow over -
My quiet nest.
   Doris Oswin

Doris Oswin lives in a council flat in a nice part of
Liskeard. She makes toys for charity, and makes jam and
marmalade for people who are sick.

Weeping Willow

They do say wisdom comes with age
the mere suggestion makes me rage
you realise in this world of old
gas and oil's worth more than gold
Get rich America.
   John Graham

John Graham was born in Glasgow in 1967. He is a research
scientist and devotes his free time to amateur studies of
history, anthropology, reading and writing poetry.

They Taught Them How

They taught them how,
To kill - maim -
Torture and love it -
But they never taught them,
How to come home,
And live.
   E. Francis

E. Francis is currently unemployed, but hopes this will get more of her work noticed.

The Beach

The beach was bare with no one there,
Only the sea, so I see,
I just wonder where everyone can be,
The sea was rough, the sand so dry,
Only the seagulls come passing by,
Empty shells were everywhere,
No one there to fill the deckchair,
Dull and grey, the sea to me
with nothing there as it should be.
A few old ships without a sail,
And all I hear the wind blowing a gale,
So quiet and bare is the beach,
Even the seaweed is out of reach,
Go to the seaside, go to the sea,
Stay home by the fire, I'd rather be.
   Eileen Durkin

Eileen Durkin is 50 years old. She is a housewife and middle aged mum of a 5 and 6 year old. She has now one poem published and hopes to go on to get a book published. She lives in Exeter, Devon.

The Bomb

Finally Holocaust happened, it seems ages ago,
Poor old world t'was struck a mighty blow.
That day the sun rose from the very earth,
Like unto a pea, bursting forth from it's pod green girth.
Breath was plucked, from the good clean air,
Giving mankind, lots of problems and care.

Looking back, people still ask how and why?,
Who dare block out God's sky.
Trees and grass ravished and burnt asunder,
Like old pirates who robbed and plunder.
Birds and bees seemed to dissapear.
Won't life feel so very queer.

Now the heat and dust has gone,
Only coldness coming on.
All who live and manage to survive,
Your alternate aim is to stay alive,
Rub the dust, and sears from your skin.
Life for you will just begin.

Don't sit down and mope and dream,
Search for a bud or a blade of green,
Man has struggled for a million years,
Overcome a billion fears.
Stood against all to see tomorrow,
Rose and fought all sorts of horror.

So let the world rest and sleep tonight,
Let the Lord have his justly rites.
Pain and punishment we must endure,
We have been worthy of this I'm sure,
Hard work, kindness, no malice employ,
And we will end strong, like the men of Troy.
George James Harvey

George James Harvey is an early retired warehouse supervisor. Born in Aldridge in Stafforshire he finds writing poetry relaxes him.

The Angry Sea

Cries of love, cries of help,
Swallowed by the raging sea,
Nets were cast, all seemed lost,
Yet nature gave sanctuary beneath the sea.

The rocks, the reefs standing fast,
Currents under the sea gave warning,
The sharks roughlessly seeking their prey,
Ships sheltering from the angry sea.

Dark clouds rolling with that silver lining,
Breakwaters holding like eagles watching their prey,
Shipwrecks sheltering life in the sea,
Yet natures creation withstanding the dangers unseen.

Drifting, moving against death unknown,
The waves with anger only brought sadness for all to see,
Only peace gave sanctuary deep down,
To the unknown world beneath the sea.

Grace and beauty of God's creation,
Across land and sea, the mountain range
Majestically looking to the sky,
The volcano erupting like the angry sea.

Dawn brought calm, peace and happiness,
Sunset brought shadows of love,
Reaching down to the depths of the sea,
Waves of anger receding,
The mountain range still guarding,
All lanes leading to those angry seas.
    Joseph Stainer Mitchell

Joseph S. Mitchell was born in Somerset and is now retired. He has always been interested in writing poems and lyrics, and has had six poems published todate.

Starvation

You can see the mist in the air as it gently creeps,
Over the makeshift homes where their occupants sleep.
Empty stomachs and vacant eyes,
Screams in the night as a child dies.
All the suffering and all the pain,
A mother's loss is anothers gain.

A scale of starvation of the likes we could never dream,
Becomes a reality on the T.V screen,
A howling child and a mother's cries,
The upturned earth where her baby lies.
And the bones stacked high marks their final place,
Where they gave up hope with the human race.

Living under a red-hot sun which shows no escape,
Their only chance of survival is tangled in red tape.
With no fertile land which could nourish a crop, '
Whenever the long awaited rains decided to drop.
A dried up river bed yields no drinking well,
And only adds to their journey on the road to hell.
Through hungry eyes too weak to cry,
They watch their brothers and sisters lay down and die.

A visting dignitary in his designer made suit,
Would rather feed them with guns than with barley and fruit,
With a promise of aid which he'll never supply,
He hasn't a thought for the thousands who'll die.
   John Dunlop

John Dunlop is 30 years old, and was born in Glasgow. He now lives in Southampton, and hopes to find a publishing outlet for a collection of poems.

Memory

You were here for such a short time,
But your memory will never fade.
Your strength and courage,
Made us all realise how brave you were,
And made me see how weak, I really am.
Your small frail body,
Hid a soul made of courage,
Which made me see you differently.
You were kind and gentle,
Even if you were in pain,
Now, I hope your burden is gone,
And now there's nothing stopping you.
Your hair will grow long and beautiful,
And your body will be strong.
You will go somewhere happy,
Where grief and pain don't exist,
We all love you, and miss you,
But your life has made a difference.
Your thirteen years on this earth has touched many,
And you will not be forgotten,
You may be dead in body,
But not in mind and soul.
   Melanie Stone

Melanie Stone is a fourteen year old student of Northfield
Upper. She wrote this in memory after the death of her
friend Lisa.

A Prayer

Starving children racked with pain,
Caused by one man, Saddam Hussein.
When will they stop him, why don't they try.
Do politics rule, must these children all die?

Freezing cold on the mountain side,
Bare feet in mud, slither and slide.
Eyes that stare, all unbelieving,
Mothers, fathers, disbelieving.

What is it with us that we let it happen
He sits in his palace that we could not flatten
When will it end, will it be too late
To save little children from their miserable fate

Though I have not prayed for such a long time
God, I ask a favour for all mankind
A favour on earth, in Iraq and Iran
Please save these people from this evil man.
   Christine Brawn

Christine Brawn is a nurse and usually writes only for her
own pleasure.

A Lonely Junkie

The room was dark and dingy
The mattress grubby and stained
He stared uncaring at the ceiling
As tiny worms wriggled around his brain.

He lay in the foetus position,
Shivering. Though sweat oozed from his pores,
Trembling, he stuck his thumb in his mouth
His arms were covered in sores.

Snakes slithered over his body
There were spiders all over his bed
He tried to pull himself together
But the hammers were bashing his head.

He fixed the tourniquet, and found the needle
Pierced his vein and waited for the high
His heart surged with sheer exhilaration
And like the screaming gulls he could fly.

They found him in the morning
Contorted on blood splattered flags
He would never again take another 'fix'
He was carried away, in black plastic bags.
   Phyllis Thelma Taylor

Phyllis Taylor lives in the village of Wales, near Sheffield.
A member of the Rotherham Writers' Group she has had
success with short stories and poetry. She retired ten years
ago.

Obsession

I want to die!
Why? So I can escape from it.
That which is devouring my mind,
And has caused my soul to split.
So, here in my darkened room
I lie naked, listening to their moaning,
Still in my flesh ridden tomb,
Feeling faint towards the mourning.

That empty bottle beside my bed
Emptied by an obsession
That twists a knife in a brain that's already dead,
To make a point, no one will listen.
My only friend is a heart which screams.
And a spirit that cries with my sadness,
And that shies away from the life that darkens my dreams,
Leaving nothing but cold, aggressive blackness.

So, as I head towards that flattest of lines
And the life force within begins to fade,
The last few pictures that enter my mind
Are of a world left behind
That might enjoy better days.
  Andrew Hale

Andrew Toby Giles Hale, a Midlander now domiciled in
Torbay is currently reading for a degree at Plymouth. He
is working on his first poetry collection and has ambitions
towards novel writing.

Life

Little child inside you keep
All curled up and fast asleep
Baby moves and mother smiles
A wonderful look is a mother with child

Now that movement has all stopped
Because in your arms your child you rock
Sweet and loving, touching too
The child you hold is a picture of you.

And now my friend
Or shall I say mum
Your life has started
It's just begun.
  Theresa Marston

Theresa Marston has four sons and works part time as a
cleaner. The above poem was inspired by Matthew Andrew
Maher.

The Bricks Behind the Door

As each room bares a door, as each door holds a key
Each key being the master to what is considered 'Free'
But if bricks in abundance, I, each exit replace
Then each exit I try, a brick wall, I face?
When each door I now meet, bares the words, 'No Escape'
As freedom is laced, by each brick I then drape
As the door to life's path, determination then proves
Extracted is confusion, direct from life's grooves.

If a wall of recluse I'm determined to build
Each exit I take, with self made material is filled
As only 'I' know the substance, by which that material is
made
Then only 'I' then that substance, for freedom can trade
As each exit gets shorter, by each brick less, I make
The pathway to freedom, I then undertake
As I begin to dispose of each brick in my mind
Alas! unexpected, an escape route, I find?
    Jeanette Walls

Jeanette Walls, aged 35, is a housewife from Glasgow. She
has two young children and enjoys putting to rhyme everyday
subjects which she feels society is ignoring or most of all,
has forgotten.

Mans Final Destination

The day will dawn
When this, our world
Will finally cease to be
When all man's work
Will be destroyed
And everyone shall see

Who shall stand
On that great day
Before the living Lord
Not the sinner
Not the slothful,
Fire shall be their reward

It is the just and holy man
Who shall a blessing receive
For he alone did face the foe
For he alone did believe

For all mankind did go astray
And believed the wicked lie
Man listened to the evil one
And for this he shall surely die

But those who sought their God in peace
And followed after love,
Shall see the heavenly Jerusalem
And live for ever up above

So come and seek the Lord today,
And knock upon His door!
Come now while there is left some time
And life shall be yours for evermore.
  Alicia Anne Griffiths

Alicia Anne Griffiths is a classical pianist and has had poems
published in various anthologies.

Insanity

Twisting, turning, falling, burning,
Into the hell gotton pit of loneliness...loneliness
Thinking, people normal people, living
laughing, brightness burning,
In my life only darkness rules.

People shouting, brightness, angels, soon be
there with you my Lord,
Only no He hath no sinners. God is bright,
Hell is dark. Black smoke, acrid, fires
burning, twisting turning...into life once more.

Mother, nurses, why so simple? Pity, scared
Not on social, thinking undone. Lovers leaving
Friends conceiving, if only he hadn't gone
No time now, only limbo, people coming
People going, no love showing...
Soon be there with you my Lord.
   Tina Wood

Tina Wood is an 'A'level student from Hemel Hempstead.
She spends most of her spare time writing poetry and short
stories, and is hoping to devote more time to it after
graduation.

Granpa Jam

Hey, Look it's Granpa Jam,
stuffing his creaky face,
with a mass of spam.
Telling all those stories,
About the war.

Children, come and listen,
he'll make your little,
eyes glisten.
And your heart will,
feel plenty sore.

What is it today,
the one where he shot the Jap,
who was trying to pray?
or the one where he was shot,
in the leg?

No, it's a different one,
one we've never heard before,
full of lots of fun.
Where the queen inscribed something,
on his wooden peg.

Oh no, I've heard it before,
and everytime he tells it he,
changes it more and more.
You shouldn't believe,
a thing that he says.

'Come, my child.' says Granpa Jam,
'Come and listen while you can.'
as he finished his spam.
'Cause I am going soon,
and you'll miss me in,
future days.'
   Robin James Napier

Robin James Napier, although originally an actor, has written
a few plays and quite a few poems. He hopes to have his
collection, 'The Perceptions Through an Eyeball', published
soon. He lives in a very cold flat.

The Dead They Walk You Know?

We are of the night,
You know the dead they walk,
They voyage to the light,
Reminisce when they talk.

They remember things that could have been,
The coronation of the Queen,
Of people-snakes that betrayed and hiss,
Of the treasured yet bungled, illicit first kiss.

But the journey's a long one,
Don't worry there'll be time to talk,
Just don't expect a second coming,
'You can't ride in the Merc. Sir,
I'm afraid you'll have to walk'.

They took me from my bed,
Told me of the walking dead,
And of when the moon would retreat from my gaze,
Turned blood-red through the fiery haze.

I don't preach, I'm not a hippy,
I don't wear flowers in my hair,
But mine's a burden I have to bear,
It's a cross I could, but should never share.

Through these words please listen,
Stop talking at the back,
Time's nearly over, the bell's about to ring,
But it doesn't mean you shouldn't nod your head,
At the pretty girls when they pass by,
All I'm saying is,
'If you don't laugh you're gonna have to cry'.
  Terry McSweeney

Terry McSweeney lives and works in Chatham, Kent. He
writes poetry and short stories in his spare time, soon he
is going to University hoping to study a film and drama
course.